Writers
at Work

The Short Composition

Ann O. Strauch

CAMBRIDGE
UNIVERSITY PRESS

32 Avenue of the Americas, New York, NY 10013–2473, USA

Cambridge University Press is part of the University of Cambridge.

It furthers the University's mission by disseminating knowledge in the pursuit of education, learning and research at the highest international levels of excellence.

www.cambridge.org
Information on this title: www.cambridge.org/9780521544962

First published 2005
Reprinted 2016

Printed in Italy by Rotolito Lombarda S.p.A.

A catalogue record for this publication is available from the British Library

Library of Congress Cataloging in Publication Data
Strauch, Ann O.
 Writers at work. The short composition / Ann O. Strauch.
  p. cm.
 ISBN 978-0-521-54496-2
  1. English language- Textbooks for foreign speakers. 2. English language-
Composition and exercises. 3. Report writing–problems, exercises, etc.
 I. Title: Short composition. II. Title.

PE1128.S883 2005
808'.048–dc22

                                          2005042183

ISBN 978-0-521-54496-2 paperback

Art direction and book design: Adventure House, NYC
Layout services: Page Designs International
Illustration credits: Rick Powell, pages 5, 20, 38, 58, 76, 94, 112, 130, 142, 156, 160, 162, 16

Table of Contents

Chapter Contents

Begin with the Basics

CHAPTER 1   Writing about a Person

* The items in this column refer to the titles of the
information boxes that appear throughout the book.

CHAPTER 2 Narrating a Personal Experience

CHAPTER 3 Providing Examples

CHAPTER 4 Supplying Reasons

CHAPTER 5 Supporting with Parallel Points

CHAPTER 6   Interpreting Quotations and Proverbs

CHAPTER 7 Writing a Summary

CHAPTER 8 Responding to Nonfiction

CHAPTER 9 Critiquing Fiction

Introduction

THE *WRITERS AT WORK* SERIES

The *Writers at Work* series takes beginning to high intermediate-level writing students through a process approach to writing. The series is intended primarily for adults whose first language is not English, but it may also prove effective for younger writers or for native speakers of English who are developing their competence as independent writers in English.

- *Writers at Work: From Sentence to Paragraph* prepares beginning to high beginning students to write grammatically accurate, topic-related sentences as the basis for an introduction to paragraph writing.

- *Writers at Work: The Paragraph* prepares high beginning to low intermediate students to write well-developed paragraphs using a variety of organization types.

- *Writers at Work: The Short Composition* prepares low intermediate to intermediate-level students to put together several paragraphs to write well-constructed and well-edited short compositions.

- *Writers at Work: The Essay* prepares intermediate to high intermediate students to write fully-developed essays with an introduction, body paragraphs, and a conclusion. Upon completion of this book, students will be ready for more advanced-level academic writing courses.

The approach

Competence in writing comes from knowing *how* to write as much as from knowing *what* to write. That is why the *Writers at Work* books are organized around the process of writing. They teach students about the writing process and then guide them to use it as they write. We believe that once students understand how to use the writing process in writing sentences, paragraphs, short compositions, and essays, they will gain the confidence they need to advance to more complex writing tasks.

In teaching writing to lower-level students, there is always the danger of sacrificing creativity in order to achieve accuracy, or vice versa. The *Writers at Work* books guide students through the writing process in such a way that their final pieces of writing are not only expressive and rich in content, but also clear and accurate.

ABOUT *WRITERS AT WORK: THE SHORT COMPOSITION*

Chapter structure

Each chapter is divided into the following five parts:

I Getting Started

Students are stimulated to think about the topic of the chapter. They generate ideas that they can use later in their writing.

II Preparing the First Draft

Students organize, plan, and write their first draft.

III Revising Your Writing

Students analyze sample paragraphs and compositions, learn about key elements of writing, and apply those principles to the revision of their first draft.

IV Editing Your Writing

Students are introduced to selected aspects of grammar. They edit their writing for accurate grammar and write their final drafts.

V Following Up

Students share their writing with each other. Finally, they fill out a self-assessment form, which allows them to track their progress as writers throughout the course.

Key features

- The book begins with an introductory section, "Begin with the Basics," which introduces students to the writing process and to the basic elements of a short composition, including format, main idea, the body and supporting details, conclusions, and titles. This section lays the foundation for the chapters that follow.

- The nine chapters of the book present common organizational patterns and types of writing used in personal and academic writing. All of the activities and exercises in a chapter relate to the pattern or type of writing. In this way, students are able to apply what they learn in their own writing.

- The book makes extensive use of sample compositions. These have been chosen for their representative nature and their engaging content. The activities in the book guide students through analysis, revision, and editing of these compositions as preparation for their own writing.

- It is important that students collaborate and interact when learning how to write. Collaborative tasks and peer feedback activities in the text make learning to write manageable and enjoyable.

- "Sharing Your Writing" activities round out the steps in writing, providing a high-interest activity that underscores the communicative goal of writing.

Acknowledgements

Writers at Work: The Short Composition would not have been possible without the help and support of innumerable people.

At Cambridge University Press, the greatest measure of gratitude goes to Bernard Seal, commissioning editor, for his steady devotion to the project and for his talent for keeping me on track toward developing the highest quality writing text possible. The results of his attention to overall coherence and detail shine out on every page. Many thanks, too, to the project editor, Helen Lee; and to the copyeditor, Linda LiDestri. For her invaluable work in providing the manuscript with consistency and clarity, I also want to thank freelance development editor, Jennifer Bixby, whose warmth, patience, and on-target input were always much appreciated. Special thanks as well to Jill Singleton, series co-author, who offered warm camaraderie and helpful ideas throughout the project.

Thanks are also due to Don Williams, the compositor, for his meticulous work in producing the typeset copies of the manuscript and to the designers at Adventure House.

I am grateful to the following reviewers for their thoughtful criticisms and helpful suggestions: Randee Falk; Joe McVeigh; Catherine Salin, Columbus Torah Academy; and Larry Sims, University of California at Irvine, Extension.

At El Camino College in Torrance, California, I have always appreciated the warm support and helpful comments of my fellow instructors in the ESL Department. I may owe my deepest gratitude, however, to the many ESL students who have contributed the delightful sample compositions for the text. They have provided the greatest gift in offering their heartfelt hopes, dreams, and life experiences on paper. They have been the true source of inspiration for me in writing this text.

Finally, I am ever grateful to my family: Walt, Mark, and Reyna, for their patience, their unwavering confidence in me, and especially their talent for tickling my funny bone.

Begin with the Basics

In this section, you will become familiar with some basic concepts in writing. You will learn how to format and write paragraphs and short compositions, using a process approach to writing. You can use this section as a reference during the course, or you can study it in detail before you do your first writing assignment.

A Paragraph format

THE PARAGRAPH

A *paragraph* is a group of sentences about one main idea.

Look at the diagram below, which shows the shape and format of a typical paragraph. Notice that the first line of the paragraph is indented.

Practice 1

Which of the following represents correct paragraph format? Circle the number.

1 A paragraph is a group of sentences about one main idea.
It is a good idea for you, a developing writer, to put the main idea in the first sentence.
The body of the paragraph then expands on the main idea with specific, supporting details.
The paragraph usually ends with a conclusion.

2   A paragraph is a group of sentences about one main idea. It is a good idea for you, a developing writer, to put the main idea in the first sentence. The body of the paragraph then expands on the main idea with specific, supporting details. The paragraph usually ends with a conclusion.

3 A paragraph is a group of sentences about one main idea. It is a good idea for you, a developing writer, to put the main idea in the first sentence. The body of the paragraph then expands on the main idea with specific, supporting details.
    The paragraph usually ends with a conclusion.

PARAGRAPH FORMAT

Here are some tips on how to format a paragraph.

Handwriting

1 Indent the first sentence of every new paragraph. Start the first sentence at about ½ inch to the right of the left margin line.

2 Continue writing to about ½ inch from the right edge of the page on every line.

3 When you start a new sentence, leave some space between this sentence and the sentence before it. Keep writing on the same line, if possible. Don't go down to a new line for each new sentence.

Using a computer

1 To indent the first sentence of a paragraph, press the *tab* key once. Then start typing your sentence.

2 Leave margins on the left and right edges of your paper. On a computer, these margins are usually automatically set at about 1¼ inches from each side.

3 When you start a new sentence, do not use the *enter* or *return* key on your computer. Just add two spaces and then start the next sentence. As you come to the end of a line, the computer will automatically start a new line.

Practice 2

What are the three format problems in the paragraph below?

> Lately, I have been unhappy with my job as a cashier at McBuns.
> First, the hours are very hard for me.
> I work from 3:00 in the afternoon to 11:00 in the evening, and I have trouble getting up the next morning for class.
> Next, the pay is miserable.I am making only twenty cents above minimum wage.
> Last, the people I work with are unfriendly.They never smile or want to have a pleasant conversation.It is time to look for a new job.

1 _____

2 _____

3 _____

Practice 3

Write the sentences in *Practice 2* in correct paragraph format.

B Short compositions

THE SHORT COMPOSITION

A short composition states and develops one main idea. If the short composition is just one paragraph, that paragraph will include the main idea, supporting ideas and details, and the conclusion.

Sample 1

This sentence states the main idea. This sentence presents a supporting idea. This sentence gives details about the supporting idea. This sentence gives more details. This sentence presents another supporting idea. This sentence gives details about the supporting idea. This sentence gives more details. This sentence presents another supporting idea. This sentence gives details about the supporting idea. This sentence gives more details. This sentence states the conclusion.

In a short composition with several paragraphs, the main idea is in the first paragraph. The conclusion is in the last paragraph.

Sample 2

This sentence states the main idea. This sentence presents a supporting idea. This sentence gives details about the supporting idea. This sentence gives more details. This sentence gives more details.

This sentence presents another supporting idea. This sentence gives details about the supporting idea. This sentence gives more details. This sentence gives more details. This sentence gives more details.

This sentence presents another supporting idea. This sentence gives details about the supporting idea. This sentence gives more details. This sentence gives more details. This sentence states the conclusion.

Practice 4

Read the following short composition. Then, answer the questions below it by giving the sentence numbers.

Wrong Number

[1]Phone calls for the wrong number seem to come at very bad times. [2]For example, a few weeks ago I was enjoying a snack and a movie when suddenly the phone rang. [3]As I was running to the phone, I tripped over the dog and found myself on the floor. [4]When I got to the phone and picked it up, a strange voice asked for Julie.

[5]I also get wrong numbers when I'm in the bathtub. [6]For example, last weekend I was enjoying a nice hot bath when, of course, the phone rang. [7]At

first, I didn't move, but then I worried that it might be an important call. ⁸I grabbed a towel and rushed to the phone, just to hear a voice ask, "Is this Fran's Homestyle Restaurant?"

⁹Sometimes I get a wrong number when I'm cooking. ¹⁰Last night the phone rang while I was preparing dinner, and the person calling couldn't believe that he got the wrong number. ¹¹He started arguing with me about names. ¹²I hung up furiously and rushed back to my burned dinner. ¹³Well, I've had enough, so from now on I will let my answering machine pick up phone calls.

Adapted from a composition by Valerie Redon Gabel

1 Which sentence states the main idea of the composition? _____

2 Which sentence gives the first supporting idea? _____

3 Which sentences give details about the first supporting idea? _____

4 Which sentences give additional supporting ideas? _____

5 Which sentence states the conclusion? _____

Practice 5

The following sentences give instructions for a science experiment showing kinetic energy. Kinetic energy is energy of motion. The sentences are not in correct order. Number the sentences to show the correct order. The first one has been numbered for you. Then, on a separate piece of paper, write the sentences in correct paragraph format.

_____ **a** Measure the temperature of the sand.

_____ **b** Then fill the cup one third full of sand.

_____ **c** Measure the temperature of the sand again.

_____ **d** Shake the sand inside the cup for one minute.

__1__ **e** The following experiment demonstrates kinetic energy.

_____ **f** At the end, you will discover that the sand is warmer.

_____ **g** Start with a large paper cup with a lid, some sand, and a thermometer.

II | PARTS OF A SHORT COMPOSITION

A The main idea

> ### GENERAL AND SPECIFIC IDEAS
>
> The main idea of a short composition expresses a general idea. In order to write an effective main idea sentence, you need to distinguish between a general idea and a specific idea.
>
> **General idea:**   a wonderful flight on Breeze Airlines
>
> **Specific ideas:**   a wide selection of in-flight music and movies
> quick ticketing and check-in
> excellent food and service

Practice 6

Each list below contains one general idea and four specific ideas. For each list, draw a circle around the letter of the general idea. The first one has been done for you.

1 a reading
  b going to movies
  c bowling
  (d) weekend entertainment
  e watching television

2 a crime
  b pollution
  c crowds
  d disadvantages of cities
  e the high cost of housing

3 a an excellent salary
  b a great new job
  c health insurance
  d flexible hours
  e company products for lower prices

4 a fresh air
  b advantages of camping
  c beautiful mountains
  d away from city crowds
  e cheap

5 a marriage
  b children
  c good job
  d goals for the future
  e college degree

Practice 7

Read the specific ideas in each list. Then, write a general idea for each list. The first one has been done for you.

1 *my ideal job*
   good pay
   friendly co-workers
   flexible hours
   located close to home

2 _____
   warm weather
   job opportunities
   plenty of fun things to do
   friendly people

3 _____
   to live closer to my relatives
   to enjoy city life
   to get a job in the computer industry in Toronto
   to live in a multinational city

4 _____
   reading mystery novels
   playing soccer
   going to action movies
   drawing cartoons

5 _____
   to gain useful knowledge
   to please my parents
   to get a better job
   to meet interesting people

6 _____
   can share all my secrets with her
   enjoy the same interests, such as jazz music
   has a fun sense of humor
   makes me feel good about myself when I'm feeling down

THE TOPIC AND THE COMMENT

The main idea sentence contains two key parts: the topic and the comment.

The *topic* is the subject or general idea the writer is presenting.

The *comment* is the writer's opinion, emotion, or other idea about the topic.

My flight on Breeze Airlines was very enjoyable.
topic   comment

Practice 8

Read the following main idea sentences. In each one, underline the topic and circle the comment. The first one has been done for you.

1 I had a (wonderful time) on <u>my vacation in Cancun last summer</u>.

2 Smoking is dangerous for several reasons.

3 Walking is one of the best exercises known to humankind.

4 I have three favorite pastimes on weekends.

5 Ms. Jenkins, my writing instructor last semester, was a great teacher.

6 Living in a big city offers many advantages.

7 When a person gets married, he or she needs to accept new responsibilities.

8 It is not easy to be a good parent.

9 Small cars offer many benefits.

10 It's convenient for a college student to own a laptop computer.

Practice 9

Write a main idea sentence for each of the following paragraphs. Include a topic and a comment in your sentence.

1 _____

First, the pay is excellent. I make much more than I did in my previous job, and I have a company car. Next, I really enjoy the people I work with. They are always friendly and helpful. Last, I have a good chance for advancement in the company. My boss told me that he would like to give me a promotion within the year. For all these reasons, I think I will stay with the company Acme Boxes for a while.

2 _____

Before we got a table, we had to wait for forty-five minutes. During the entire time we waited, the hostess kept telling us it would be only five more minutes. Once we sat down, I saw that my water glass was dirty. The waiter brought a clean glass, but I got the feeling that he was mad at us for the rest of the evening. Even the food was disappointing. The vegetables and the chicken were overcooked. I will never listen to my boss's recommendation for a restaurant ever again.

3 _____

The store has a large number of sofas to choose from. They have styles you cannot find at most other stores. Also, the salespeople are patient and helpful. If you do not know exactly what you want, they will give you lots of information and let you take your time to decide. Most important, the prices are good. The store says that it has the lowest prices in town. I really recommend the store Sofa So Good for anyone shopping for a new sofa.

B Supporting ideas

> **THE BODY**
>
> The *body* is the largest part of a composition. It provides supporting ideas and details to explain and develop the main idea. The body of a composition comes after the main idea and usually has several sentences.

Practice 10

Circle the letters of the supporting ideas in each list. The first one is done for you.

1 **(a)** One thing I like to do is work in my garden.
   b I enjoy several activities on my days off.
   (c) Another activity I enjoy is going to movies.
   (d) My favorite activity is going on picnics with my family.

2 a It is close to the border so I can visit Mexico often.
   b San Diego is a great place to live.
   c The weather is great.
   d It has plenty of interesting places to visit with the family.

3 a Mouth, throat, or lung cancer rates are higher in smokers than in nonsmokers.
   b Heart disease is more common in smokers than in nonsmokers.
   c Lung disease strikes smokers more than nonsmokers.
   d Smokers have a variety of health problems.

4 a I miss my mother's warm words of advice.
   b I often think about the fun I used to have with my friends.
   c I really miss my native country, Syria.
   d What makes me the saddest is being away from my family at holiday time.

5 a The servers are friendly.
   b The food is delicious.
   c The dining room is pleasant.
   d The Velvet Noodle is a great place to eat.

6 a Spanish is an easy language for an English-speaker to learn.
   b Spanish words are spelled just like they sound.
   c Many Spanish vocabulary words are similar to English words.
   d It is easy to find Spanish speakers to practice conversation with.

7 a My suitcase did not arrive at the airport with me.
   b I had a terrible flight on Bay Airlines last summer.
   c The food was awful.
   d The in-flight movie didn't work.

8 a I dislike standing in long lines.
   b I hate rush-hour traffic.
   c The constant noise bothers me.
   d I have several complaints about living in crowded cities.

C Supporting details

USING DETAILS

Good writers use details to support their ideas and to make their writing more interesting. In the body of your composition, use sentences which support your main idea with specific details.

In these examples, an idea was made more specific and clearer by adding details.

> I drove my car on the freeway.
> I raced my new Honda on the 405 freeway.

> One student was rude to some others.
> The high school boy yelled at the younger boys, "You're stupid!"

Practice 11

Read the title and the main idea below, which are followed by pairs of supporting ideas. Read each pair of supporting ideas, and circle the letter of the one that gives better specific, supporting details.

Fond Memories of a Starry Night

I really love the memories that I had with my mother, especially one from the hot nights when we used to sleep in the backyard.

1 a The sky was beautiful, and my mother and I spent many hours looking at it. It was really the most beautiful sky I have ever seen. My mother thought so, too.
 b I remember that the dark sky had plenty of stars, and there was a full moon. The stars and moon gave us their full brightness.

2 a The view was gorgeous, and we saw many things in the sky.
 b Sometimes we saw shooting stars crossing the sky until they got lost in the distance.

3 a My mother told me stories until I fell asleep.
 b My mother sat by my side, telling me stories about a princess, until I fell asleep.

4 a The next morning, noise woke us up, but the most beautiful feeling was being with my mother.
 b The next morning, I was surprised to be woken up by the rooster's crowing. But the most beautiful feeling was having my mother next to me.

Adapted from a composition by Gladys Monge

Practice 12

Rewrite the following sentences. Substitute the underlined ideas with specific details. The first one is done for you.

1 My father greeted her with a gift.

My father greeted his younger sister with a beautifully wrapped birthday present.

2 I like music.

3 My computer wasn't working right.

4 The car was dirty.

5 The cat relaxed.

6 The sales clerk was rude to me.

7 At the birthday party, my neighbor's children were very polite.

8 Last week, I had car trouble.

9 The movie I saw last week was scary.

10 I enjoyed my vacation.

D The conclusion

A *conclusion* ties together the entire composition and gives closure. This sample composition does not have a conclusion.

My Job Dissatisfaction

Lately, I have been unhappy with my job as a cashier at McBuns. First, the hours are very hard for me. I work from 3:00 in the afternoon to 11:00 in the evening, and I have trouble getting up the next morning for class. Next, the pay is miserable. I am making only twenty cents above minimum wage. Last, the people I work with are unfriendly. They never smile or want to have a pleasant conversation.

Without a conclusion, the reader wonders "And so . . . ?" Read the following common types of conclusions and examples that would work well for the paragraph above.

Types of conclusions

1 A restatement of the main idea

There is no doubt about it: I really do not like my job.

2 A summary of the points

I just cannot accept the terrible hours, the low pay, and the unfriendly atmosphere.

3 A look to the future

It is time for me to look for another job.

4 A related thought that grows out of the body

I wish I could quit this job tomorrow.

5 A combination of several types of conclusions

There is no doubt that I really do not like my job, so it is time for me to look for another one.

Practice 13

Write conclusions for the following compositions.

Composition A

Money and Happiness

Having money does not guarantee happiness. When I was younger, my family was not rich, but we were happy for many years. Then one day, unexpectedly, my mother inherited my grandmother's fortune. Soon we were arguing about what to do with the money. We fought over the jewelry until everyone was very upset and unhappy. I wanted us to be the way we were before we got so rich. Luck changed for us, though, when we came to this country. We lost all of our belongings on the trip here. However, little by little, we got back what we had lost and needed most: our love for each other.

_____

_____

_____

Adapted from a composition by Ngi Nguyen

Composition B

Honesty Is Best

"Honesty is the best policy." This famous saying from Miguel de Cervantes' *Don Quixote* means that we have to be honest in all situations. I agree, especially because of what happened to my grandfather about three years ago. He got sick, and his doctor secretly told us my grandfather had cancer. His doctor put him in the hospital, but he did not tell my grandfather the truth right away. During the first three months in the hospital, my grandfather was more and more tired, and the cancer just kept getting worse. Then the doctor told him the truth — that he had cancer and would live for only a few months. I thought my grandfather would not be able to accept the truth, but a strange thing happened. He began enjoying his life. He was even able to leave the hospital sometimes to do whatever he really wanted to do. To my surprise, my grandfather lived for another year. _____

_____

_____

Adapted from a composition by Tomo Wakamatsu

Composition C

> ### Culture Shock
>
> I started experiencing culture shock shortly after I arrived in this country. In Vietnam, when young people speak to an older person, they have to be very respectful. They have to use different ways of speaking to older people. If a young person uses the wrong words with an older person, the older person will get upset. But English does not have different ways to speak to older people, and I didn't understand this when I first arrived in this country. I felt uncomfortable when I talked with my teacher, for example, because the word "you" sounded so disrespectful. Instead of using the word "you," I began to say "Teacher! Teacher!" When my friends laughed at me, I started using the word "you" with teachers, even though I still felt it was impolite.
>
> _____
>
> _____
>
> _____
>
> _____
>
> *Adapted from a composition by Huyen Tran*

E Titles

GUIDELINES FOR TITLES

Every composition needs a title. The *title* introduces your composition and should catch the reader's attention before he or she starts reading. Even though the title appears first, many writers prefer writing the title after they write the composition.

Follow these guidelines for titles.

1 Center the title on the top line of the paper.

2 Capitalize the first and last words of the title, as well as the most important words (the words with the most meaning).

3 Use a capital letter after a colon (:).
    Parenting: Life's Biggest Challenge

4 Do not capitalize the following words.

    Articles: a(n), the

    Coordinators: and, but, or, so

    Short prepositions: in, on, at, to, for, with, from

There are two exceptions to this rule.

- Always capitalize the word if it is the first or last word in the title.

    A Childhood Home Revisited

- The first word after a colon is always capitalized.

    My Favorite Uncle: A Brief Description

5 If a quotation appears in the title, use a capital for the first word in the quotation.

    An Interpretation of "No man is an island"

6 Do not write a sentence as a title. Do not use a period at the end of a title.

7 Do not underline a title.

Practice 14

Rewrite each title correctly.

1 my biggest mistake ever

_____

2 Hope For The Future.

_____

3 A Terrifying Midnight Boat Ride

_____

4 I had a disappointing welcome in Chicago.

_____

5 My Dreams For The Future

_____

6 A True Saying: "you get what you pay for"

_____

7 A summary and reaction to the story "one exit"

_____

8 My first and last trip to Disney World

_____

Practice 15

Write a title for each of the following compositions.

1 Title: _____

Mother love is one of the finest gifts I received as a child. I still remember clearly when I was six years old and had the measles. I had to be isolated from the rest of the family. I was sad about being alone away from my brothers and sisters, but Mom patiently told me why it had to be that way. She not only took care of me for the next two months, but she also cheered me up and read to me for long hours. She even slept in my room on the floor, and when I woke up, she stayed awake with me. I hope I can be as good a mother to my own children some day.

Adapted from a composition by Claudia Ortiz

2 Title: _____

When I remember the moonlit nights in Vietnam from twenty years ago, I am filled with wonderful memories of the countryside. I used to enjoy sitting in a chair in my garden on warm evenings and watching how the moon lit nature up and turned it into a beautiful oil painting. The river looked like a silvery finger in the upper corner of the painting. In the middle, points of light would dot the leaves of the trees. And in my own garden at the bottom of this painting, I could see the face of the moon in tiny pools of water.

To accompany this visual beauty, the wind played a romantic song to me. The breeze brought to my nose the smell of the rice field behind my house. Sometimes, my tongue could even taste salt on my lips, salt brought from the sea by the gentle wind.

Often, when the fog slowly rolled in, nature's painting turned pale and dreamy, and the moon turned into a soft glow. Then the cold wind would push me back into the warmth of my house. Now in my new country, whenever I see a full moon, I remember Vietnam.

Adapted from a composition by Hoa Pham

STEPS IN PROCESS WRITING

When you write a composition, your goal is to communicate your ideas clearly to your reader. In process writing, you will write several versions, or drafts, of your composition. You will make changes and improvements in each draft. Your final draft will clearly communicate your ideas.

Here are seven steps that writers typically go through during the writing process.

Step 1: Selecting a topic
Step 2: Planning and organizing
Step 3: Writing the first draft
Step 4: Revising
Step 5: Proofreading and editing
Step 6: Writing the final draft
Step 7: Sharing your writing with others

Following the process approach, however, does not mean that you must follow the steps in exactly that order.

Imagine a circular building with six rooms, as in the illustration below. You go in through the entrance into a room called "Selecting a topic." You go in and out of the rooms to your left and exit the building through the room marked "Writing the final draft." However, notice that once you go into a room to your left, you can always come back through the center of the building to a room on your right. This is because writing does not always go smoothly forward. Sometimes writers need to go back as well as forward.

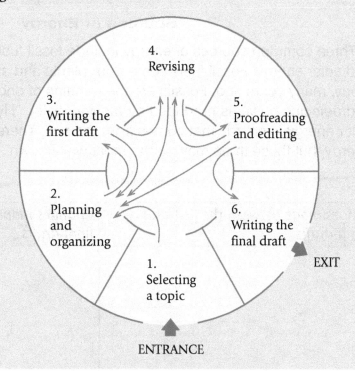

Practice 16

Read the following three drafts. Then complete the chart, identifying the types of changes and corrections made between the first and second drafts, and between the second and final drafts. Look, for example, for changes in content and grammar.

First draft

Energy

There are three comon source of energy. Fossil fuels come from plants and animals that die many, many years ago. Fossils are the remains of once living things. Hydroelectric power is produced by moving water. Solar energy is energy that come from sun. There are another sources of energy as well.

Second draft

Sources of Energy

Three comon source of energy include fossil fuels, hydroelectric power, and solar energy. Fossil fuels come from plants and animals that die many, many years ago. Fossils are the remains of once living things. Next, hydroelectric power is produced by moving water. Hydro means water. Last, solar energy is energy that come from sun. There are another sources of energy, but these three may be the most well-known.

Final draft

Sources of Energy

Three common sources of energy include fossil fuels, hydroelectric power, and solar energy. Fossil fuels come from plants and animals that died many, many years ago. Fossils are the remains of once living things. Next, hydroelectric power is produced by moving water. "Hydro" means water. Last, solar energy is energy that comes from the sun. There are other sources of energy, but these three may be the most well-known.

Changes made between the first and second drafts	Changes made between the second and final drafts

Writing About a Person

I f you look around in class, you will probably see a lot of new faces – people like you, who are eager to improve their English. You may not know it yet, but you probably share many other common interests.

For the writing assignment in this chapter, you will interview one of your classmates – someone that you don't already know. Then you will write about your classmate.

A Read sample compositions

As you read the following compositions, think about what makes each person stand out as an individual with a unique personality. When you have finished reading, share your ideas with the class. Also say which of the four people seems to be most like you and why.

▌Sample 1

A New Friend with a Playful Sense of Humor

Victor Carrasco is in my ESL writing class this semester. He is from Veracruz, Mexico, and he has been here for two years. His major is electronics, and when I asked him why, he responded that he has always enjoyed learning about how things work. When he was a child, he would take apart radios and clocks just to see how they worked. He added with a smile, though, that his mother did not like his hobby.

Victor said he really likes the United States. I asked him why, and he said that it is easier to get an education here than it is in Mexico. At the time he arrived, he could not speak English very well and had some trouble communicating. He was able to learn more English by taking classes at night.

When I asked him what his dreams were for the future, he smiled, pointed upward, and said that he dreams of being up in the sky. I was surprised by his answer. I did not understand what he meant. Then he laughed and said that he wanted to be in a jet flying to distant countries such as Spain and Japan to see how other people live. His eyes sparkled when he spoke of traveling and seeing other countries.

Victor impressed me as a kind and funny guy. He told a lot of jokes during the interview, and I laughed a lot. With his friendly personality and natural sense of humor, he will have a lot of success in his education and in his travels to other countries. I am glad to have a new friend like Victor.

Adapted from a composition by Takejiro Hirayama

Sample 2

Nigisty: Woman of Service

I met Nigisty in my writing class this semester. She came from Eritrea, East Africa, five years ago. She now lives here in California with her husband, son, daughter-in-law, and granddaughter.

In Eritrea she lived a peaceful and prosperous life. Then one night her comfortable lifestyle was taken away from her when the communists took power in her country. Luckily, she was able to escape, but she had to leave some of her family behind, including her mother.

Nigisty is taking three courses at the college during the day and is working as a nurse's aide in the evening. She wants to become a nurse because she loves to help people. In Eritrea, she provided many health services to people. For example, she delivered many babies and helped wounded soldiers. Also, she assisted AIDS and HIV-positive patients. Even though nursing can be difficult at times, Nigisty loves her work and is happy to be of service to people who need help and comfort.

In Nigisty's spare time, she exercises at a gym and follows her religious faith with her family. In this way, she said, she keeps her body, mind, and spirit healthy.

I am truly impressed with Nigisty's generous spirit. Giving to others gives her life meaning. I can see this in her warm smile and glowing eyes when she speaks of her heart's desire – service to others. I admire the way she has come through hard times and has still kept her warm, giving nature.

Adapted from a composition by Sue Paik

Sample 3

The Dairy Queen from Mongolia

Suren Nadmid is my classmate this semester in ESL 53A. "I'm from Mongolia," she said and smiled at me. In addition to a really cute smile, Suren has beautiful, shiny hair and lovely, dark brown eyes. Even though she is only sixteen years old, there is a strong light and determination in her eyes.

continued

Suren came to study in the United States because she thinks the educational system is better here than it is in her country. When her English is better, she is going to study economics at a university.

When I asked Suren if she missed her family, she answered, "I make a phone call to my family every week." She went on to say that she was determined to study economics in the United States despite her loneliness.

However, she knows how to relieve her loneliness. She is crazy about movies. Last weekend she went to three movies. When she told me about the movies, her face became happy again, and I could see the innocent youth in her face return.

Eventually, she wants to go back to Mongolia to manage her father's dairy food company. She said that dairy products are very important in Mongolia. As she spoke about this, she looked proud. She is not an only child, however. She has two brothers. One of them is ten years old, and the other is studying law at a Mongolian university. In a few years, her father is going to give his company to one of his three children. At this point in our interview, her shy smile widened and showed her confidence and ambition. She reminded me of a queen.

Although Suren is charming and delicate looking, she is strong in her beliefs. From our conversation, I felt sure that such a powerful girl will make the future of Mongolia better. I certainly hope she is successful.

Adapted from a composition by Chiyako Tasai

Sample 4

A New Family in a New Country

Ghadeh is a new friend in my composition class this semester. Ghadeh came to the United States from Amman, Jordan, two years ago. She came with her husband, Mody, her father, brother, and other family members.

Ghadeh and Mody now live three miles from the college. She is expecting a baby in four months, and she is excited about becoming a mother. When she isn't studying, she spends her free time watching TV and reading books on child care. Ghadeh's career goal is to become a successful hotel manager.

Ghadeh likes the United States. I asked her why, and she said that women have more freedom in this country. For example, here, a woman can live alone, and it is easy for a woman to have a career outside the home. All in all, Ghadeh believes that she will have new opportunities here.

I really enjoyed interviewing Ghadeh. She's a warm, friendly person, and talking with her was a pleasant experience. I'm sure that she will make all of her dreams for life in the United States come true. Although Ghadeh comes from a different culture than I do (I come from Peru), I believe that Ghadeh came to the United States for the same reason that I did – to have a better future.

Adapted from a composition by Jeanette Blake

B Determine your audience

> **AUDIENCE**
>
> Before you write, you need to identify your audience. Your *audience* refers to the person or people who will read your finished composition. Knowing your audience helps you write appropriately for that specific person or group. For example, if your audience includes your classmates, your instructor might suggest an informal style.

Who is your audience for this composition? _____

C Select a topic

For this assignment, your topic will be your interview partner. If possible, your partner should be a person you do not already know.

Write the name of your partner. _____

D Interview your partner

Follow these steps to interview your partner.

1   Write a list of questions to ask in your interview. Here are some topics you may want to ask about.

Basic background information
- Place of birth
- Family
- Places your partner has lived

Interests and opinions
- Hobbies, sports, and other pastimes
- Opinions about the school, city, or country that you are in
- Opinions about events in the news
- Things your partner has a strong opinion about: family, friendships, politics, religion, health, success, or other topics
- Goals or plans for the future

2   Interview your partner using your list of questions. Feel free to include other questions and explore other topics that you and your partner find interesting.

3   Take notes during your interview. You will use them later when you write your composition.

THE FIRST DRAFT

The first piece of writing that you produce for your composition is called a *first draft*. When you write your first draft, you will focus on organization and content. Don't worry about making grammar and spelling mistakes. You will have a chance to revise and edit later.

A Identify types of information

A COMPOSITION ABOUT A PERSON

Three types of information should be included in your composition about a person.

- Basic background information, such as the person's country of origin, family information, and educational or career goals

  He is from Veracruz, Mexico, and he has been here for two years.

- Personal information, such as interests, opinions, and goals for the future

  When I asked him what his dreams were for the future, he smiled, pointed upward, and said that he dreams of being up in the sky.

- Your reaction to the person, such as whether you find him or her sad, intelligent, or funny

  Victor impressed me as a kind and funny guy.

Practice 1

Read the following sentences, some of which are from the sample compositions. Identify the type of information in each sentence. Write the letter of the correct answer on the line. The first one has been done for you as an example.

> B = **B**asic background information
> P = **P**ersonal information, such as interests, opinions, and goals
> R = **R**eaction the writer had to the person interviewed

_B_ 1 Asha is originally from Somalia, and she came to this country two years ago.

_____ 2 Thuy likes this country because the living standard is high.

_____ 3 It felt wonderful to see Thuy's smile; it told me that she was a happy person.

_____ 4 With Victor's friendly personality and natural sense of humor, he will have a lot of success in his education and in his travels to other countries.

_____ 5 Tran is very interested in engineering, and he dreams of being a successful engineer in the future.

_____ 6 I can understand how frightening it must be to escape without your family and to try to adapt in a foreign country alone.

_____ 7 To earn money, she does sewing at home, which she enjoys because she likes creating useful and attractive clothing.

_____ 8 Ghadeh believes that she will have new opportunities here.

_____ 9 I am truly impressed with Nigisty's generous spirit.

_____ 10 She now lives here in California with her husband, son, daughter-in-law, and granddaughter.

Your turn ↪

Identify the different types of information you have in your interview notes. Use the same abbreviations as in *Practice 1* (*B, P,* or *R*) and write them in the margin of your notes.

B Make a rough outline

ROUGH OUTLINES

Before writing your first draft, you need to plan ahead and organize your ideas. Some experienced writers organize their ideas in their heads. As a developing writer, it will be helpful to organize your ideas on paper. One common way to organize is to make a rough outline. Many student writers find this technique the easiest and most effective way to organize their ideas.

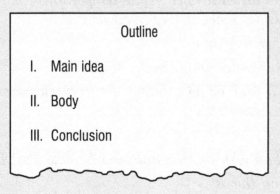

```
                    Outline

    I.   Main idea

    II.  Body

    III. Conclusion
```

Read the example of a rough outline on the next page.

I. MAIN IDEA

Who?   *Faiza Fazeli*
Where? *ESL composition class*
When?   *this semester*

II. BODY

Basic background information

from Iran
came to the United States 3 yrs. ago
lives with her parents and younger brother

Personal information, such as interests, opinions, and goals

enjoys science, especially biology, anatomy, and chemistry
wants to go to a state university and become a dentist
wants to get married some day, after becoming a dentist
misses her hometown, but likes living in this country
loves to take walks in nature
favorite place to hike and enjoy nature: Grand Canyon
went there last summer, and she and brother hiked to bottom and back
went to Las Vegas after the Grand Canyon, but didn't like it
feels sad that some people misunderstand her religion
devoted to her religion and to her family, but respects others' religions
her religion — promotes peace and responsibility to the family
doesn't believe in drinking alcohol

Writer's personal reactions

Faiza has a gentle and sensitive nature.
I'm glad a person such as Faiza with her gentle temperament is planning to become a dentist. She would make a very good dentist.
I enjoyed learning about her religion.
We have a lot in common: love of family and nature.
We may get together for a walk or hike during the next vacation.

III. CONCLUSION

I've never had a conversation with anyone from the Middle East before.
I learned a lot of interesting things.
I enjoyed our time together.

Your turn ↶

Using the information from your interview, make an outline similar to the one on the right. Then complete it to help you plan and organize your ideas. Write key words and ideas in your outline.

> **I. MAIN IDEA**
> Who?
> Where?
> When?
>
> **II. BODY**
> Basic background information
>
> Personal information, such as interests, opinions, and goals
>
> Your personal reactions
>
> **III. CONCLUSION**

C Compose the main idea

> ### THE MAIN IDEA
>
> The first sentence in a short composition often states the main idea.
>
> When you are writing about a person that you have interviewed, a clear main idea sentence answers these questions: Who? Where? When?
> - **Who** you interviewed: Quang Ly
> - **Where** you interviewed the person: in my ESL writing class
> - **When** you interviewed the person: this semester
>
> Main idea: Quang Ly is one of my classmates in my ESL writing class this semester.

Practice 2

Using the following information, write a sentence for the main idea.

> Who: Ilya Glazunov
> Where: in Composition A
> When: this fall

Main idea sentence: _____

Your turn ↶

Write the main idea sentence for your composition. Include information about who, where, and when.

D Organize the body

THE BODY

Here is information that should be in the body of a short composition about a person.
- Basic background information
- Personal information, such as interests, opinions, and goals
- Reaction the writer had to the person interviewed

Practice 3

Reread the student compositions at the beginning of this chapter, and label the three types of information in each one.

> B = **B**asic background information
> P = **P**ersonal information, such as interests, opinions, and goals
> R = **R**eaction the writer had to the person interviewed

Your turn ↶

Use your rough outline to help you write the body of your composition. Focus on the most interesting information about your partner, and present him or her as a unique individual.

E Write a conclusion

THE CONCLUSION

The *conclusion* ties the entire composition together. It gives closure. Often it gives the writer's strongest impression.

In a composition based on an interview, the writer can give his or her personal reaction to the interview.

> I admire the way she has come through hard times and has still kept her warm, giving nature.

> From our conversation, I felt sure that such a powerful girl will make the future of Mongolia better. I certainly hope she is successful.

Practice 4

In the following pairs of sentences, one is a conclusion and one is not. Circle the letter of the conclusion.

1 **a** I will always remember Seynab's courage.

　b It took her three years to get a visa for the United States, but she finally succeeded.

2 **a** In the second week of the semester, I met and interviewed Thuy Pham in my ESL writing class.

　b I am really glad I had the chance to talk with Thuy Pham.

3 **a** I was surprised to learn that Shinya plays so many sports.

　b I learned many interesting things about Shinya's interests and look forward to hearing about how his competitions go this year.

4 **a** Paulo is very determined to get a college degree.

　b I was impressed by Paulo's determination to get a college degree and feel sure he will succeed.

5 **a** From our interview, I learned that Maria is a very active member of our college community.

　b Maria is very athletic and plays on the college's basketball team.

Your turn

Look back at your rough outline and find the information that you labeled *R* in *Your turn* on page 25. Use this information to help you write the conclusion of your composition.

F Put together the first draft

As you have worked your way through Section II, you have written all the pieces that you need for a short composition: the main idea, the body, and the conclusion. Put these pieces together to create the first draft of your composition. Then add a title. Read about titles in *Begin with the Basics* on pages 14–15.

REVISING

Revising means improving the content and organization of your draft. When you revise, you can add material, delete material, or move material from one place in the composition to another.

Use the following editing marks when you revise.
- Carets (∧) to show where to insert material
- Lines to cross out material
- Circles and arrows to show where you're moving material

>   *this semester*
>   Victor Carrasco is in my ESL writing class. His major is electronics, and when I asked
> him why, he responded that he's always enjoyed learning about how things work. When he
> was a child, he would take apart radios and clocks just to see how they worked. He added
> with a smile, though, that his mother did not like his hobby. He is from Veracruz, Mexico,
> and he has been here for two years. Veracruz is a large city on the east coast of Mexico.

A Analyze supporting details

Practice 5

When writing a composition, one common mistake is not developing or explaining the ideas in the body with enough specific, supporting details. Read the two versions of the paragraph that follow. They are from a student composition. Which one has better specific, supporting details? Be prepared to explain your choice.

Version 1

> Tomoe has a boyfriend from another culture who speaks two languages. He is in the military. He's fairly young. I could tell that she loves him very much because when she talked about him, she seemed very happy. She misses him a lot when he's away. After she told me about him, she asked me about my boyfriend. When I told her about him, she showed interest in hearing about him. We both have special feelings for our boyfriends.

Version 2

> Tomoe has a Spanish-speaking boyfriend who is in the military and travels a lot. His name is Emanuel, and he's twenty years old. I could tell that she loves him very much because when she talked about him, her eyes lit up and her face glowed. She misses him a lot when he's away. After she told me about Emanuel, she asked me about my boyfriend. When I told her about him, she listened attentively and asked me questions about him. We both have special feelings for our boyfriends.

Practice 6

Using your imagination, add specific details to complete the following composition.

A Successful Future Ahead

I met and interviewed Miguel Jimenez in my ESL writing class a week ago. Miguel was born in Mexico and finished one year at the University of Mexico. After he came to this country, he got a job _____ _____. He's married.

Miguel is trying to decide between two majors: _____ _____. This is his first semester at a U.S. college. He's taking all ESL classes, so he has some time before he has to make a final decision about his major.

When I asked him what he enjoys doing, he answered that he likes to work out in a gym when he can because _____. He also likes to watch _____ movies and to take short trips with his wife to places such as _____.

Then I asked Miguel about his plans for the future. He said that he is planning to move from his apartment to _____. He wants to have good friends that he can trust, and he'd like to have one or two kids some day. Also, _____.

I asked Miguel which he liked better — the United States or Mexico. He said he preferred _____ because _____ _____.

I enjoyed interviewing Miguel. His friendly personality and honesty put me at ease. I respect his desire to build toward a comfortable life for himself and his family. I have no doubt that he will be successful.

Adapted from a composition by Mohammed Jaber

B Benefit from peer feedback

PEER FEEDBACK

A useful activity for revising is to exchange drafts with a classmate and give each other feedback. When you give feedback, you offer comments, suggestions, and impressions. This activity gives you valuable practice in analyzing a draft for possible improvement. You will also receive suggestions from your partner about possible improvements for your draft.

Carefully consider your partner's feedback, but make your own decisions about what to revise. It's a good idea to wait several hours or overnight before making revision decisions, so that you can evaluate your writing with a fresh mind.

Exchange drafts with a partner. Read your partner's draft and check it using the *Revision Checklist* below. At this point, do not check grammar. Then give your partner feedback and discuss the composition.

REVISION CHECKLIST ☑

☐ 1 Does the draft have any places that are unclear?

☐ 2 Is the draft organized clearly, according to the outline form on page 27?

☐ 3 Does the body need more supporting details?

C Make revision decisions

Using the *Revision Checklist,* decide on the changes you want to make. Mark the changes in your draft. If necessary, ask the person you interviewed for additional details or information.

D Write the second draft

Write the second draft, making changes and improvements.

EDITING YOUR WRITING

A Use editing symbols

> ### EDITING
>
> *Editing* means looking for and correcting errors. When you edit your final draft, check for errors in grammar and format.
>
> - Cross out any words or letters you want to delete.
> - Use a caret (∧) to show where to add words.
> - Check any spelling that you are unsure of.
> - Check any punctuation that you are unsure of.

Practice 7

Look at the editing symbols in the first two sentences of the paragraph below. Then find and mark the four corrections needed in the last two sentences.

>   Nigisty ^{*is*}∧ taking three courses at the college and is working as ∧^{*a*} nurse's aide in the evening. She want^{*s*}∧ to become a nurse̸ because ∧^{*she*} loves to help people. In Eritrea, provided many health services to peoples. For example, she deliver many babies and help wounded soldiers.

B Edit for subjects and verbs

> ### SUBJECTS AND VERBS
>
> In academic and other formal writing, every sentence and every clause must contain at least one subject and verb.
>
> - The *subject* tells what the sentence is about. The subject can be a noun or a pronoun.
>
>   <u>I</u> interviewed Zahid Memon in my ESL writing class this semester. <u>Zahid</u> is from Pakistan. <u>He</u> came to this country two years ago in January. <u>His uncle</u> picked him up from the airport.
>
> - There is a special class of subjects called *filler subjects*. *It* and *there* are filler subjects.
>
>   <u>It</u> was a cloudy, rainy evening when Zahid arrived. <u>It</u> was very cold. <u>There</u> were several accidents on the freeway, so <u>there</u> was a lot of traffic.

- The *verb* supplies the action or state of being for the subject. A verb may consist of one word or several words (for example, one or more auxiliaries plus the main verb).

    The following Saturday, Zahid's aunt and uncle <u>took</u> him to see the sights in the city. They <u>showed</u> him the beautiful buildings downtown. They also <u>spent</u> some time at Stanley Park. Zahid <u>was</u> very impressed.

    Now, two years later, Zahid <u>has seen</u> a lot of tourist spots. To give a few examples, he <u>has visited</u> Niagara Falls, Banff National Park, and New York City. Also, he <u>has been saving</u> his money for a trip to San Francisco.

Practice 8

Edit the following composition for missing subjects and missing verbs. Use a caret (∧) to show where to add words. There are 9 missing subjects and 6 missing verbs.

Laundry with a Smile

¹José Gutierrez is one of my classmates in my ESL writing class this semester. ²He to this country from Mexico six years ago. ³At present, lives with his mother in Wilmington and works for ETO Gas.

⁴When I asked José what he's interested in, he had lots of answers. ⁵He wants to be a mechanic because likes to fix cars. ⁶If his friends ask him to fix their cars, he very happy to do so. ⁷To my surprise, he learned the skill of mechanics by himself. ⁸Also wants to have a medical laboratory and do research on diseases.

⁹José spends a lot of his free time with his girlfriend. ¹⁰Like to go to the movies or shop at the mall. ¹¹When he talked about her, looked especially cheerful. ¹²In addition, he to watch sports such as soccer and basketball. ¹³Once in while, he plays soccer with his friends. ¹⁴Curiously, likes to do the laundry. ¹⁵He says that doing the laundry a kind of sport. ¹⁶That made me wonder. ¹⁷What kind of sport could it be? ¹⁸For me, is an unpleasant sport! ¹⁹I wish I could enjoy doing my laundry.

²⁰From this interview, José impressed me as a hard-working guy with a lot of interests. ²¹He just about every day in addition to going to school. ²²Sounds so boring to me to spend so much time working and going to school. ²³But he still many other interests that he somehow finds time for. ²⁴I'd like to model myself after him in the way that he keeps a busy schedule and still finds time for many

---

other activities. [25]Also, admire his devotion to his girlfriend.

[26]All in all, José seems to be enjoying life. [27]The picture of José that may stay in my mind the longest, though, is the one of him doing his laundry with a smile on his face.

Adapted from a composition by Ken Yamamoto

C Benefit from peer feedback

PEER FEEDBACK

Checking a partner's draft gives you valuable practice in proofreading and editing. In addition, your partner can give suggestions for possible changes for your own draft. Most students agree that it is easier to see errors in other students' writing than in their own.

Meet with a partner and exchange drafts. Read your partner's draft, and check for subject or verb errors. When you get your paper back, correct your errors.

D Write the final draft

Write your final draft, making the revisions and edits you have noted on your second draft.

V FOLLOWING UP

A Share your writing

SMALL GROUP READ-AROUND

There are many advantages to sharing your writing with others in your class. It gives you the opportunity to communicate your ideas and get to know others in your class. In a Small Group Read-Around, you work in a small group and read each person's composition. Each time you read a partner's composition, select one idea that you find notable or interesting. Do not comment on the organization or the grammar. After you have read all of the compositions, share with the whole group what you find interesting about each one.

Do a Small Group Read-Around. Form a group of approximately four students, and read and comment on each other's compositions.

B Check your progress

After your instructor returns your paper, look for patterns of strengths and weaknesses. Complete the *Progress Check* below. Then you can focus on building your strengths and work on your weaknesses.

PROGRESS CHECK

Date: _____

Composition title: _____

Things I did well in this composition:

_____

_____

Things I need to work on in my next composition:

_____

_____

_____

Narrating a Personal Experience

Most people have had countless personal experiences that have affected them in some way. Have you had an experience that gave you the feeling of total peace? Have you had a terrifying experience? Have you had a funny experience in a new culture?

For the writing assignment in this chapter, you will write a narration about a personal experience that has affected you in some specific way.

GETTING STARTED

A Read sample compositions

As you read the following compositions, decide on the writer's strongest emotion or opinion about the experience. Discuss your answer with the class. Say if you have had a similar experience.

Sample 1

RVs

    A funny thing happened to my family last spring vacation. We wanted to rent an RV (recreational vehicle) for a short trip. While we were discussing plans, my grandmother called the phone company to get the number of a place that rented RVs. With a broad smile on her face, she handed me the phone number. I hugged Grandma and thanked her.

    I called the number right away. The person who answered announced in a cheerful voice, "Thank you for calling RVs. What can I do for you?" Glad to have the right place, I asked for the location and directions. The woman gave me directions and said I would see a really big sign with "RVs" on it. "Oh, good!" I said, and continued, "By the way, what is the biggest you have?" She answered, "Super size." I thanked her, said goodbye, and hung up. Then I reported what I found out to my family.

"They have super size," I said. "How big is super size?" asked my sister. "Let's go and see," I suggested. We were both excited about making all the plans for the trip.

We followed the directions the lady gave us, but we couldn't find the RV rental company. After almost two hours of driving around and looking, we parked on the side of the street.

Discouraged, I told my sister that I was tired of looking, and I wanted to give up and go home. At that moment, my sister yelled, "Oh, my gosh, I think I got it!" I responded, "No kidding?" "Hey, yeah, take a look up there ahead!" It was then that I finally saw the really big sign of a fast-food restaurant that read "Arby's."

After this experience, I don't rely anymore on information Grandma gets on the phone. Also, when I call for information myself, I make sure about the spelling.

Adapted from a composition by Sang Park

Sample 2

Polar Bear Mechanics

I'll never forget my first few moments at the Anchorage airport. I was ten years old at the time, and my parents were moving from Korea to Alaska for their new jobs. I was very excited about living in a new country, but I was totally surprised by what I saw.

As soon as the airplane arrived in Anchorage, I eagerly looked out the window. One word describes what I saw: *white*. All I saw was white snow all over the ground. Even the trees at the edge of the runway were covered with white. The next thing I saw was a mechanic servicing an airplane and wearing a huge, white coat to cover his entire body and face. He looked more like a polar bear than a person.

I started to feel desperate. I kept trying to tell myself positive things about Alaska, picturing fun activities such as catching fish and climbing icy mountains, but another voice in my mind told me, "Hyung Jung! Your life in Alaska is going to be miserable! You can't have fun outside wearing a polar bear coat!" I kept telling myself that it would all be okay. Maybe I could even find new indoor hobbies. I was trying to think positively, but it was difficult.

With all these worries, I walked toward the airport terminal. "Anchorage Welcomes You," it said on the arrival door. As I entered the building, people greeted me with big smiles. The warm welcome by the people made me feel a little better. But I'll always remember the sight of the white polar bear mechanics on the snow-covered runway of the Anchorage, Alaska, airport.

Adapted from a composition by Hyung Jung Lee

Welcome to the Big City

I had the most terrifying experience of my life two years ago when I was a newcomer to the city. I was working as a deliveryman for Dominic's Pizza, and I had to make a night delivery. The neighborhood I went to looked isolated, with almost no lights on at all.

After I delivered the pizza, I started back to the car with the money in my hand. As soon as I stepped out of the apartment building, a tall man suddenly stood in my way and tried to grab the money, saying with a rough voice, "Give me the money!" I stepped back, but then I felt someone behind me grabbing me around the neck. I was trapped. The first guy threatened me again and kept demanding the money. However, I could not talk because the other guy was squeezing my throat. I was very frightened because I knew that I couldn't fight them.

Of course, they took the money, which was about fifty-five dollars. Before they left, though, they pushed me down onto the sidewalk. Somehow, I made it back to my car and drove away.

The fear from that night will always stay with me, but the experience taught me how to act in this kind of situation. The key is to keep cool and to stay away from isolated places at night.

Adapted from a composition by Esteban Andiola

Peace at Mount Kyaik-Hti-Yeo

When my family and I climbed Mount Kyaik-Hti-Yeo to see one of the most famous Buddhist pagodas in Myanmar, the former Burma, I discovered total peace. It was the first day of our vacation, so we were looking forward to a day without stress. On the way up the mountain, we passed small souvenir shops and resting places. We met other people climbing with us and had some pleasant conversations. We passed waterfalls and watched monkeys playing in the trees. When we arrived at the top, we were tired, but happy. However, the gentle music from the pagoda gave us new strength.

After a little while, we entered the pagoda to pray. Some people were pouring water on the statue of Buddha to wash away their sins. Others were meditating. Visitors decorated the pagoda with candles and beautiful, fresh flowers. After I prayed, I looked around and saw the huge, green mountains surrounding me. The beauty of both the pagoda and nature brought complete peace to my mind.

Later that evening, we returned down the mountain. We used a flashlight to light our way through the stillness. As we hiked down, we reminded each other of the beauty and peace we had experienced. I want to keep this peace in my heart forever.

Adapted from a composition by Ni Ni Lay

B Select a topic

Read the following topics and select one for your narration composition.

1 A situation in which you experienced joy, peace, or other pleasurable emotion

2 An embarrassing or funny situation
(This could be a cultural misunderstanding or a language problem.)

3 A frightening or terrifying situation
(You might remember a situation from childhood or one that you had more recently. Write about a real situation, not a bad dream.)

4 A situation in which you felt proud of yourself or a family member
(Did you accomplish a personal goal? Did your child perform in a play or music recital? Did your team win an important game?)

5 A situation in which you experienced panic over a minor problem

6 Other topics: _____

C Ask yourself questions about your topic

Your turn 〰

Ask yourself questions about your topic. Complete the chart below with the questions and then write the answers in note form.

Question words	Questions	Answers
Who . . . ?		
When . . . ?		
Where . . . ?		
What . . . ?		
Why . . . ?		
How . . . ?		

D Discuss your experience with others

TALKING TO GET IDEAS

When you tell another person about your experience, you will have the opportunity to explore and develop your ideas. Your partner will also ask you questions. In this way, you will develop plenty of specific, supporting details and think of additional details.

With a partner or in a small group, take turns telling about your experience. Follow these steps.

1 Tell what your experience was and how you felt when it happened.
2 Explain what happened from one moment to the next, using specific details.
3 Ask if your experience and details are clear.

A Make a rough outline

Make an outline similar to the one on the right. Then complete it, writing key words, phrases, and ideas.

I. MAIN IDEA
II. BODY Background Action and details (Who, what, when, where, why, and how)
III. CONCLUSION

B Compose the main idea

THE MAIN IDEA

A clear main idea sentence includes a topic and a comment. In a narration, the topic is the event, experience, or situation. The comment is the writer's opinion, emotion, or other idea about the topic.

For a short composition, you can just give one comment. Look at this example.

Topic:

Who?	my family and I
What/Where?	Eritrea under communist rule
When?	October 1, 1980
Comment:	terrifying
Main idea:	October 1, 1980, was the most terrifying day of my life, when my country Eritrea came under communist rule.

Practice 1

Read sample composition 4 on page 40. Follow these steps.

1 Underline the main idea.

2 Write the topic: _____

3 Write the comment: _____

4 Circle words in the rest of the narration that remind you of the comment.

Practice 2

Circle the letter of the best main idea in each of the following groups. Be prepared to discuss the reasons for your choices.

1 a It took me two years to learn how to ride a horse.
  b The first time I tried riding a horse was one of the most frustrating days of my life.
  c I learned how to ride a horse shortly after I moved to the mountains.

2 a I had an exhausting but exciting time hiking to the bottom of the Grand Canyon last summer.
  b Last year when I visited the Grand Canyon, I hiked all the way to the bottom of the canyon.
  c Hiking to the bottom of Grand Canyon was exhausting.

3 a My first attempt at painting a room turned out to be disastrous.
  b One day last spring my husband and I painted the baby's room.
  c I've painted three rooms in my house over that past year, and I've hated every minute of it.

4 a In my first week in this country, I was embarrassed over a silly mistake I made while I was shopping for a birthday present at the mall.
  b I hate embarrassing situations.
  c In my first week in this country, I had a wonderful time shopping at the mall, but my fun was spoiled when I made a silly mistake.

5 a Last Monday evening while I was watching TV, the telephone rang.
  b Last Monday evening while I was watching TV, I got a phone call that made me angry.
  c Last Monday evening while I was watching TV, the telephone rang, and a strange voice asked me, "Are you the lady of the house?"

6 a I like to talk with my friends on my cell phone.
  b My cell phone often loses its connection while I'm in the middle of a conversation with a friend.
  c I was very annoyed last week when my cell phone lost its connection while I was talking to my friend.

Your turn ℛ

Write the main idea for your narration. Include the topic and the comment.

C Provide background information

BACKGROUND INFORMATION

For some narrations, you may need to start with some brief background information. The *background information* is usually after the main idea and before the action of the story starts. This information is important for understanding the story. However, limit your background information to just what is necessary.

In the following example, the background information is underlined.

> The first time I went ocean fishing with my uncle, I was scared to death. <u>I was only nine years old when Uncle David convinced my mother that I was old enough for fishing out on the ocean.</u> Uncle David and I left early the next morning . . .

Practice 3

Underline the background information in the excerpts from the compositions at the beginning of the chapter.

1   A funny thing happened to my family last winter vacation. We wanted to rent an RV (recreational vehicle) for a short trip. While we were discussing plans, my grandmother called the phone company to get the number of a place that rented RVs. With a big smile on her face, she handed me the phone number. I hugged Grandma and thanked her.

2   I'll never forget my first few moments at the Anchorage airport. I was ten years old at the time, and my parents were moving from Korea to Alaska for their new jobs. I was very excited about living in a new country, but I was totally surprised by what I saw.

3   I had the most terrifying experience of my life two years ago when I was a newcomer to the city. I was working as a deliveryman for Dominic's Pizza, and I had to make a night delivery. The neighborhood I went to looked isolated, with almost no lights on at all.

4   When my family and I climbed Mount Kyaik-Hti-Yeo to see one of the most famous Buddhist pagodas in Myanmar, the former Burma, I discovered total peace. It was the first day of our vacation, so we were looking forward to a day without stress. On the way up the mountain, we passed small souvenir shops and resting places.

Your turn

Decide if your narration needs more background information. If so, add additional notes to your rough outline.

D Use time order to organize ideas

ORGANIZING USING TIME ORDER

The body of a narration composition is normally organized using time order. *Time order* means that the events and actions follow the order in which they occurred in time. Time words and expressions help the reader follow the action in time order.

> <u>After</u> I delivered the pizza, I started back to the car with the money in my hand. <u>As soon as</u> I stepped out of the apartment building, a tall man <u>suddenly</u> stood in my way and tried to grab the money, saying with a rough voice, "Give me the money!" I stepped back, but <u>then</u> I felt someone behind me grabbing me around the neck. I was trapped.

Practice 4

Read the following narration, "My First and Last Camping Trip." Write numbers in the blanks to indicate the correct time order for the sentences. The first sentence is numbered for you.

My First and Last Camping Trip

I had a frightening experience on a camping trip in Armenia a year ago. My family wanted to go camping. I was afraid of the idea of sleeping outdoors in a tent in the mountains, but I made up my mind to go anyway.

_____ a When I looked through the keyhole, I saw a big brown bear nearby.

_____ b The next day, I decided that I never wanted to go camping again.

___1___ c When we got to the campsite, a man told us to be careful of the bears that came out of the woods at night.

_____ d I had a great time, until the third night.

_____ e I was so frightened that I decided to spend the rest of the night in the restroom.

_____ f My heart was racing, and I prayed that the door was strong.

_____ g When I got to the restroom, I heard sounds coming from the woods.

_____ h It was about 3:00 A.M., and I had to go to the restroom, which was on the top of the hill, approximately thirty yards away from our tents.

_____ i While I was watching, the bear came closer to the restroom and started sniffing around it.

Adapted from a composition by Tiopa Techiryan

Your turn ↺

Look at your rough outline. Organize the actions and details into time order. Then write the body of your composition, using time words or expressions to make the time order clear. Focus on content and organization. You can correct grammar later when you revise.

E Include plenty of action and specific details

USING DETAILS

The body of a narrative composition relates the action, using specific details to make the action come alive for the reader. These details support the main idea and help the reader picture the action in his or her mind, moment by moment.

Practice 5

Read the first part of "Stuck in the Mud," which was adapted from a student composition. For the rest of the narration, read each pair of sentences, and choose the one that describes the action more clearly or gives better details. Be prepared to identify the words in each answer that make the sentence clearer and more detailed.

Stuck in the Mud

On the way from the Grand Canyon to Phoenix, Arizona, two years ago, my husband and I had a wonderful experience when our car got stuck in the mud. This may sound strange, but let me tell you my story. We decided to take a short cut on a dirt road. We saw some black clouds forming ahead, but we did not think much about them. We didn't realize that we were heading for trouble.

1 a Within ten minutes, it started to rain hard, with strong winds.
   b Soon the weather turned very bad, and there was rain.

2 a Huge amounts of dirty water turned the road into a river, and we got stuck in the soft mud.
   b Lots of water came down; there was water everywhere, and we could not drive any further.

3 a We struggled to get out for a long time, but nothing happened no matter what we did.
   b We struggled to get out for six hours, with no success, and nobody passed by.

4 a When it started to get dark, we became worried and soon afterwards lost hope.
   b When it started to get dark, we felt very bad and later we felt even worse.

5 a Then we saw a light somewhere in the distance.
   b Then we saw some light coming from the other side of the hill.

6 a With new hope, we climbed up over the muddy hill and met a young couple.
   b Feeling better, we went to look for the people and met a young couple.

7 a Luckily, they had a four-wheel drive truck and pulled our car out of the mud.
   b Luckily, they had a truck and they helped us.

8 a After that, they were very kind and offered to help us in any way they could.
   b After that, they offered to accompany us until we reached the paved road.

9 a We had several more problems along the way, but each time they helped us.
   b We got stuck again many times along the way, but each time they pulled us out.

10 a I was happy when our terrible experience was finally over.
   b I was happy when I finally saw the lights of civilization.

Thanks to the kindness of this couple, our vacation ended happily. Since then, we have developed a wonderful friendship.

Adapted from a composition by Teruyo Tsuchiya

Your turn ↶

Check the body of the composition that you wrote in *Your turn* on page 47. Do you have plenty of action and specific, supporting details? How can you add more specific, supporting details?

F Write a conclusion

THE CONCLUSION

A *conclusion* ties the entire composition together and gives closure. A narration may conclude in one or more of the following ways.

- A restatement of the main idea

   As we hiked down, we reminded each other of the beauty and peace we had experienced.

- A related thought, such as what you learned or how you changed

   The fear from that night will always remain with me, but the experience taught me how to act in this kind of situation. The key is to keep cool and to stay away from isolated places at night.

- A look to the future

   I want to keep this peace in my heart forever.

Practice 6

Follow these steps to analyze the composition below and its conclusion.

1 Underline the main idea and circle the comment.
2 Put parentheses around the background information.
3 Underline the action verbs in the body.
4 Put two lines under the conclusion.
5 Identify what type of conclusion it is: a restatement, a related thought, or a look to the future.

The Most Terrifying Day of My Life

¹The most terrifying day of my life started when my daughter had a terrible accident with hot cooking oil two years ago. ²I had gone to school to register for classes. ³By the time I got home I was very hungry and tired. ⁴I started preparing French fries, and just when the oil had gotten hot, my daughter came to ask me for water. ⁵As I turned to give her the water, I bumped the handle of the pan, and the hot oil went all over her legs. ⁶I still remember her screaming from the pain. ⁷I looked at her legs, and the skin looked like hot melted wax. ⁸In shock, I rushed her to the hospital.

⁹At the hospital, a doctor treated her burns, while I walked back and forth in the waiting room, crying and praying. ¹⁰To make matters worse, though, an administrator at the hospital refused to believe that it was an accident. ¹¹This made me even more upset.

¹²My daughter and I did not get home until the next day. ¹³Although I was finally able to go home with my daughter, the scars on her legs will always remind me of that terrifying day.

Adapted from a composition by Gema Martinez

Your turn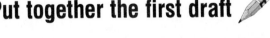

Write a conclusion for your narrative composition. What type of conclusion is it – a restatement, a related thought, or a look to the future?

G Put together the first draft

As you have worked your way through Section II, you have written all the pieces that you need for a short composition: the main idea, the body, and the conclusion. Put these pieces together to create the first draft of your composition. Then add a title.

REVISING

When revising your writing, you make changes to improve the content and organization of your draft. You can add material, delete material, or move material from one place to another.

A Delete irrelevant material

IRRELEVANT MATERIAL

When writing a composition, a common mistake is including irrelevant material. Sentences that do not support or explain the main idea are *irrelevant*. When you revise your writing, check for irrelevant material. Delete sentences that do not support the main idea.

In the excerpt from a composition below, the writer has crossed out irrelevant sentences that do not support the comment.

> After a little while, we entered the pagoda to pray. Some people were pouring water on the statue of Buddha to wash away their sins. Others were meditating. Visitors decorated the pagoda with candles and beautiful, fresh flowers. ~~There were lots of bees around the flowers.~~ Everyone's face reflected the harmony and tranquility all around us. ~~There was a young teenager, however, who spent all his time playing games on a small handheld computer. It was annoying, but I tried to ignore him.~~ After I prayed, I looked around and saw the huge, green mountains surrounding me. ~~The mountains reminded me of an enjoyable vacation I took last summer in Colorado.~~ The splendor of both the pagoda and nature brought complete peace to my mind.

Practice 7

Follow these steps to analyze the composition on the right.

1 Draw lines through the seven irrelevant sentences, and be prepared to discuss why these sentences are not helpful.
2 Underline the main idea and circle the comment.
3 Put parentheses ( ) around the background information.
4 Put brackets [ ] around the action section. Which is longer: the background information or the action? Put a star in the margin next to the longer section.
5 Underline the conclusion.

A Disappointment in My Brother

[1]Last summer I was disappointed in my younger brother because of his bad judgment. [2]My brother came from Austria to visit my family and me for a month during his school vacation. [3]My parents had paid for his plane ticket to visit us, so it didn't cost him anything. [4]After a month with us, he was planning to visit a few places in the United States, such as Disneyland, before returning to Austria for the next school term. [5]He was about to graduate, and he already had his driver's license.

[6]One day my brother was in the backyard playing with our nephew. [7]I could see them from my bedroom. [8]I was reading a science fiction novel at the time. [9]They were kicking an old ball from one end of the yard to the other, having a great time, running, kicking, and laughing.

[10]Then they went into the storage shed, and after about ten minutes my nephew looked out the half-closed door and then slowly closed it completely. [11]The look on his face made me wonder what they were doing. [12]Usually my nephew is the family clown, and he likes to make everyone laugh. [13]When they did not come out for a long time, I got curious and decided to see what was so interesting.

[14]What I saw was a horror! [15]In the middle of the shed was a fire. [16]They were burning toy cars and trash. [17]When I saw the fire, I was furious! [18]They both stood up right away and tried to block my view of the fire, but it was impossible to hide it. [19]Last year our neighbor's daughter started a fire in his shed, and the shed burned down. [20]The fire destroyed her father's camping gear. [21]I was so disappointed in my brother because he was eighteen years old and should have known better than to start a fire in a shed.

Adapted from a composition by Teresa Poteranska

Your turn ↰

Check your draft for any irrelevant material. Delete it, as necessary.

B Benefit from peer feedback

PEER FEEDBACK

When you have a classmate read your first draft, you can get useful feedback. You can find out what a reader thinks is unclear, poorly organized, or not well written. This will give you ideas about how to improve your draft.

Exchange drafts with a partner. Read your partner's draft and check it using the *Revision Checklist* below. At this point, do not check grammar. Then give your partner feedback.

REVISION CHECKLIST ☑

☐ 1 Does the draft have any places that are unclear?

☐ 2 Is the draft organized clearly, according to the outline form on page 43?

☐ 3 Is the draft free from irrelevant sentences?

☐ 4 Does the draft need more supporting details?

C Make revision decisions

Using the *Revision Checklist*, decide on the changes you want to make. Mark the changes in your first draft.

D Write the second draft

Write the second draft of your composition, making changes and improvements.

IV EDITING YOUR WRITING

A Check for past time verbs

ACTION VERBS AND TENSE

Most narrations contain many action verbs. Since a narration describes an event from the past, most of the action verbs appear in one of the past time verb forms: simple past or past progressive. A good example of a narration with a lot of action verbs is "Welcome to the Big City" on page 40.

Practice 8

Fill in the chart with examples from the sample compositions at the beginning of this chapter. Write at least three examples in each column.

Simple past regular	Simple past irregular	Past progressive (was/were + verb + ing)
Action in the past	Action in the past	Action in progress in the past
happened		

Practice 9

Edit the following narration for verb errors. There are 13 errors. The first one is marked for you.

Marcos and Carola

¹Marcos and his wife Carola usually enjoy their trips to the Baja peninsula in Mexico. ²However, three years ago, they ~~have~~ *had* an unpleasant experience while Marcos is returning from a fishing trip. ³Marcos jump from the fishing boat onto a fish in the surf. ⁴The fish struck out with its tail and cuts Marcos' foot. ⁵The cut was deep. ⁶Marcos is bleeding badly. ⁷He grab a towel and wrap it tightly around his foot. ⁸It hurt a lot. ⁹The nearest medical clinic is 45 minutes away. ¹⁰Luckily, Carola arrives soon to pick Marcos up from the boat dock. ¹¹As soon as she arrives, she helped Marcos to the truck and rush him to the clinic. ¹²At the clinic, the doctor give Marcos some medicine and stitch up his bleeding foot. ¹³Now Marcos looks very carefully before jumping out of a fishing boat.

Your turn

Check your composition for correct past time verbs. Mark any corrections.

B Include direct quotations

DIRECT QUOTATIONS

Direct quotations report the exact words that someone spoke or wrote. When you report these exact words, they must appear between quotation marks. In a narration, direct quotations provide specific, supporting details that can help the action come alive for the reader.

If the quotation is a sentence and comes before the reporting verb, change the period to a comma. If the quotation comes at the end of the sentence, use a period and place a comma after the reporting verb.

"You're right," he said.

He said, "You're right."

Periods, commas, question marks, and exclamation marks go inside the end quotation marks.

Quietly, I asked, "How can I help you?" The soldiers pushed past me and started searching the house. "Where is your husband?" they demanded. I explained that he was asleep and not feeling well. "Even if he's sick, we want him!" they shouted angrily.

Practice 10

Edit the following narration by adding quotation marks where necessary. You will need to add 5 pairs of quotation marks.

The Zebra

¹I laugh when I recall having lunch at a small Chinese fast-food restaurant with my wealthy friend several years ago. ²When we got to the restaurant, May took out her cell phone and called a guy to join us. ³As soon as he walked into the restaurant, she became a totally different person. ⁴She talked like a singing bird and smiled with special charm.

⁵We got our food. ⁶May ate very slowly and carefully because she didn't want to get her expensive white blouse dirty. ⁷During the entire time, she never stopped talking to the guy and didn't say anything to me.

⁸After I finished eating, I entertained myself by playing with a small packet of soy sauce. ⁹I squeezed the packet and rolled it between my fingers. ¹⁰When she looked over at me, she gave me an angry look and said, What if the packet opens accidentally? ¹¹I paid a few hundred dollars for this blouse! ¹²Then she whispered angrily, Stop doing that!

¹³I put the packet down. ¹⁴Then the guy picked it up and said, It's warm from your fingers. ¹⁵He and I laughed. ¹⁶To May's surprise, the guy started playing with it. ¹⁷Then he commented, Wow! ¹⁸This is sealed really tightly. ¹⁹He squeezed the package harder.

²⁰At that moment, the soy sauce squirted out of the packet like a water gun. ²¹The dark liquid shot out at the expensive white blouse, making May look like a zebra. ²²Her friend tried to say he was sorry. ²³May screamed, Oh, no! and ran to the bathroom.

²⁴Since then, every time I go to a Chinese restaurant I remember May in her zebra blouse. ²⁵It still makes me laugh.

Adapted from a composition by Heera Lee

Your turn ↩

Did you use direct quotations in your composition? Can you add any quotations? Check your quotations for correct punctuation.

C Benefit from peer feedback

Meet with a partner and exchange drafts. Read your partner's draft, and check for verb errors or errors in punctuating direct quotations.

D Write the final draft

Write your final draft, making the changes you have noted on your second draft.

V FOLLOWING UP

A Share your writing

Share your composition with your classmates by following the directions for *Traveling Compositions,* above.

B Check your progress

After you get your composition back from your instructor, complete the *Progress Check* below.

PROGRESS CHECK

Date: _____

Composition title: _____

Things I did well in this composition:

_____

_____

_____

Things I need to work on in my next composition:

_____

_____

_____

Look at your *Progress Check* on page 36 of Chapter 1. How did you improve your writing in this composition?

_____

_____

_____

Providing Examples

How many times have you found it difficult to understand what someone has said, but as soon as some examples are given, it becomes clear what the person means? Examples really help make communication clearer.

In this chapter, you will write a short composition in which you have one main idea about a person or an event. You will give three clear examples that explain and support your main idea.

A Read sample compositions

As you read each of the following compositions, notice how three examples are used to explain and support the main idea. In the margin of each sample, number the three examples.

Sample 1

My Forgetful Mother

My mother Mieko is very forgetful. For example, when she went shopping a few months ago, she left a bag with her purchase behind in a store. She didn't even discover her mistake until she got home. Then, very worried, she called the store. Fortunately, the salesperson kept it and returned it to her.

Another example happened six years ago when my mother and I were staying in a hotel in Singapore. I told her many times that the hotel room had an auto-lock feature, and that she needed to take the key whenever she left the room. One night, I left the room to get some ice from the ice machine. I thought Mother would wait for me inside the room. When I got back, she was standing outside the door. She explained, "I was worried about you, so I wanted to watch for you." I nodded and asked her to open the door. Her eyes opened wide, and a big "ohhh" escaped from her mouth.

One more example took place a few years ago, after I presented my parents with plane tickets to Hawaii for their twenty-fifth wedding anniversary. They were very excited about the trip, but my mother's forgetfulness caused a big problem. When my parents were on the airport bus, my mother discovered that she had forgotten her purse, which had cash, credit cards, and important documents. She asked the bus driver to stop the bus so that they could get off. He did so, and she and my father rushed to the terminal. From the terminal, she telephoned me and cried, "I forgot my purse at home! Please bring it to me! And please hurry!" I did, and they were able to catch a later flight.

Now I can laugh when I tell these stories about my mother, but I sure wish her memory would improve a little.

Adapted from a composition by Eriko Iizumi

Sample 2

My Tiny Big Rescuer

My cell phone makes life easier by rescuing me when I'm in difficult situations. For instance, not long ago I was preparing for a dinner party, and I had a very busy schedule. I rushed out to go to the grocery store and to do a few other necessary errands. When I got to the grocery store, I couldn't find my grocery list. I then used my cell phone to call home, and my husband read the list to me. Thanks to my tiny friend, I was able to get everything done in time.

To give another example, last summer I had an appointment with a new dentist in an unfamiliar part of town. When I made the appointment, I got some directions that seemed fairly clear. Unfortunately, I got lost somewhere along the way. I decided to park my car and use my cell phone. Then I called the dentist's office and found out that I was only two blocks from the office. Fortunately, I got to the appointment on time.

To give one last example, during the last rainy season, I left my car headlights on while I was shopping. When I returned to my car, the battery was completely dead. I used my cell phone to call for help and simply waited calmly in my car until help arrived. I think of my tiny cell phone as my big rescuer.

Sample 3

Dangerous Pets

Even though pets are enjoyable, some pets can be harmful to people or to the environment. For example, some aquarium fish collectors think that piranhas, which are dangerous fish native to South America, make interesting pets. The problem with piranhas is that if someone puts a piranha into a local stream or lake, the piranha is likely to do some damage to the wildlife.

continued

Another dangerous pet is the Madagascar cockroach, which has become popular in some Asian countries. Apparently, their size – two inches – appeals to people who like unusual pets. According to the *Los Angeles Times* (August 21, 2002), Thailand's health minister has urged stores to stop selling these giant bugs because they create a health risk if they escape. They breed quickly and are very difficult to get rid of.

Still one more example of a dangerous pet is the pit bull, a small, strong, and often-vicious breed of dog. All too frequently, the newspapers report tragedies caused by pit bull attacks on people. Occasionally, a small child is killed by a pit bull, and adults have been seriously hurt in attacks by pit bulls. The *Los Angeles Times* (August 21, 2002) reported that a pit bull attacked a mail carrier and bit off part of her nose.

It is good to live in a society that protects the freedom of the individual to have pets. However, the freedom to own dangerous pets must be limited in order to protect our freedom to live in a safe environment.

Sample 4

Stubbornness: Her Middle Name

My youngest daughter Daniela is very stubborn. One example happened two years ago when she was in preschool. She took a classmate's chair away from her, and when her teacher asked her several times to return the chair, Daniela started crying and refused to do it. Finally, the teacher had to call me because Daniela wouldn't obey her teacher, and she wouldn't stop crying. I won't forget my little girl's face when I got to the school to pick her up and saw her crying.

Another instance of Daniela's stubbornness took place last year. It was 11:30 P.M. Everybody was asleep, but for some reason Daniela woke up. She came to my bedroom and announced, "Mommy, I want to take a bubble bath now." I explained to her why she couldn't have a bath in the middle of the night, but she started to cry and scream, "I want a bubble bath!" I refused to let her have one, and after two hours of crying, she fell asleep on the living room floor. The next day I was very tired, but Daniela got her bubble bath that morning.

A recent illustration of Daniela's stubbornness has to do with getting all her homework done. Last week, she brought home an assignment to do, but she didn't want to do it. I asked her several times to at least get it started, but she refused again and again. The next day I found out that she had to stay in the classroom during recess because she had refused to do her homework. I felt sorry for her, but maybe she will learn from this.

Having a child as stubborn as Daniela is very hard for her family. Fortunately, she is less stubborn than she used to be.

Adapted from a composition by Isabel Gutierrez

B Select a topic

Read the following topics to select one for your composition. Choose a topic that brings to mind several examples. Also, make sure that you can provide plenty of specific, supporting details for the examples.

1 Examples of a certain characteristic of a person you know
(Possible characteristics: generosity, honesty, clumsiness, perfectionism, pessimism, messiness, kindness, helpfulness, rudeness, irresponsibility, friendliness, and so forth)

2 Examples of noise pollution in the city, in your neighborhood, or another specific location

3 Examples of culture shock for foreign students from one particular country or area of the world

4 Examples of good or bad government policies or laws

5 Examples of unnecessary or necessary wars

6 Examples of changing technology

7 Examples of a situation or viewpoint that is current in the news

8 Other topics: _____

C Freewrite about your topic

FREEWRITING

Freewriting is a good way to get ideas about your topic. When you freewrite, you allow your mind to explore and write freely everything that comes to mind. Do not worry about correct grammar or spelling. If you get stuck, simply write, "I'm thinking about (*my topic*), and the ideas are starting to come to me" over and over until the ideas start coming to you.

> Noise pollution in the city. I'm thinking about noise pollution in the city, and the ideas are starting to come to me. Noise. Car alarms. Motorcycles. Cars with loud music. Screaming music. Why do people like to attract attention like that? What about their hearing? My uncle says they'll go deaf. Don't they know it bothers other people? Loud music systems cost a lot, too. Some cities have laws against loud music. Barking dogs. My neighbor has a big dog that stays alone all day in a small yard. Poor dog! I feel sorry for it. Isn't there a law against barking dogs, too? If not, there should be. Barking dogs really bother me when I'm trying to study. Sometimes they wake me up at night. . . .

Your turn ↶

Freewrite about your topic. Write everything that comes to mind, and don't worry about grammar or spelling. When you finish, circle examples you can use to support your topic.

D Discuss your ideas with others

With a partner or in a small group, take turns telling about your topics. Follow these steps to discuss the ideas from your freewriting.

1 Tell what your topic is, along with your opinion or feeling about your topic.

2 Give three examples to support your topic, and explain each one in detail.

3 Ask if your examples and details clearly support your topic and your opinion or feeling.

II PREPARING THE FIRST DRAFT

A Make a rough outline

Make an outline similar to the one on the right. Then complete it, writing key words, phrases, and ideas.

I. MAIN IDEA
II. BODY EXAMPLE 1 Details EXAMPLE 2 Details EXAMPLE 3 Details
III. CONCLUSION

B Compose the main idea

THE MAIN IDEA

Remember that a clear main idea sentence includes a topic and a comment. The topic is who or what the composition is about. The comment is the writer's opinion, emotion, or other idea about the topic. Limit yourself to one comment.

Topic: A characteristic of my mother Mieko

Comment: She is very forgetful.

Main idea: My mother Mieko is very forgetful.

Practice 1

Write a main idea for each topic. Limit yourself to one comment.

1 A friend or relative
(Identify the person and give an important characteristic.)
My cousin Maggie is very kind to animals.

2 Neighbor(s)
(Identify the person or people and give an important characteristic.)
_____

_____

3 Culture shock
(Identify the person who has experienced culture shock and add a comment.)
_____

_____

4 A current event
(Select a current event or social trend to comment on.)
_____

_____

5 Technology
(Identify the specific point you want to make about technology, such as change in daily life, or effect on education or jobs.)
_____

_____

Your turn

Write the main idea for your composition. Include your topic and a comment.

C Organize examples in a logical order

ORGANIZING EXAMPLES

Two common methods for organizing examples in a composition are time order and order of importance. *Time order* means that the examples start with the one that occurred earliest in time. *Order of importance* means that the least important example appears first, and the most important, or most convincing, example appears last.

Practice 2

Identify the method each author uses to organize the examples in the following compositions. Write *time order* or *order of importance* in the blank.

Composition A: _____

Wrong Number

Phone calls for the wrong number seem to come at very inconvenient times. For example, a few weeks ago I was getting comfortable with a snack and a movie when suddenly the phone rang. As I was running to the phone, I tripped over the dog and found myself with my nose in the carpet. When I got to the phone and picked it up, a strange voice asked for Julie.

I also get wrong numbers when I'm in the bathtub. For instance, last weekend I was enjoying a nice hot bath when, of course, the phone rang. At first, I didn't move, but then I worried that it might be an important call. I grabbed a towel and rushed to the phone, just to hear a voice ask, "Is this Fran's Homestyle Restaurant?"

Sometimes I get a wrong number when I'm cooking. Last night the phone rang while I was preparing dinner, and the person calling couldn't believe that he got the wrong number. He started arguing with me about names. I hung up furiously and rushed back to my ruined cheese sauce. Well, I've had enough, so from now on I will let my answering machine pick up phone calls.

Adapted from a composition by Valerie Redon Gabel

Composition B: _____

Culture Shock in Germany

Even though my American culture and the German culture are similar in many ways, I still suffered from culture shock during my vacation in Germany a few years ago. For example, people drive very fast on German freeways because there's no speed limit. I was driving at least seventy miles per hour, but most of the traffic passed me as though I were standing still. What really made me uncomfortable, though, was that the traffic coming up behind my car honked at me impatiently.

To give another example, whenever I paid for something at a store, I would hand over my money to the cashier and then extend my open hand toward him or her for the change. But the cashier seemed to ignore my hand and put the change on the counter, leaving my open palm hanging in the air. After this happened several times, I wondered if the Germans were being unfriendly to me because I was American. Later I realized that the problem was a difference in customs.

The most dramatic example of culture shock happened when I went shopping for fruit in a grocery store. The store looked very similar to what I was used to, so I felt comfortable going about my business normally. I was selecting peaches and putting them into a paper bag, when a tall German woman ran toward me screaming angrily. I honestly didn't know what the problem was. Since I didn't speak German, I couldn't understand her or speak up for myself. I felt confused, helpless, and embarrassed. It turned out that customers are not supposed to select their own fruit. Instead, the clerk is supposed to choose it and put it into a bag for the customer. Even though these examples seem like minor incidents, all together they made me uneasy until I realized that I was experiencing a normal case of culture shock.

Your turn ↰

Look at your rough outline, and decide how you will organize your examples. Arrange them in a logical order.

D Use transition signals to introduce examples

TRANSITION SIGNALS

Transition signals are words or expressions that help the reader follow your ideas from one example to the next.

For example,
To give another example,
The most dramatic example

One example was
Another instance was
A recent illustration was

First,
Another,
Still another is

Practice 3

Underline the transition signals in the four sample compositions at the beginning of this chapter.

Your turn ↰

Decide on transition signals for your composition. Then, use your notes and your rough outline to write the first draft of the body of your composition.

E Use specific, supporting details

SUPPORTING DETAILS

In a composition, develop each example with specific, supporting details. For personal examples, explain clearly what happened using action verbs, detailed descriptions, and quotations. Give specific information, such as the time and place. If you get your information from a source such as a newspaper or the Internet, identify the source.

Look at the supporting details in the student composition below.

Another example happened <u>six years</u> ago when my mother and I were staying in a hotel in <u>Singapore</u>. I told her many times that the hotel room had an <u>auto-lock feature</u>, and that she needed to take the key whenever she left the room. One night, I left the room <u>to get some ice from the ice machine</u>. I thought Mother would wait for me inside the room. When I got back, she was standing outside the door. She explained, <u>"I was worried about you, so I wanted to watch for you."</u> I nodded and asked her to open the door. <u>Her eyes opened wide</u>, and a big <u>"ohhh"</u> escaped from her mouth.

Practice 4

In small groups, select either Composition A or B. Working together as a group, write specific, supporting details for the composition. Use your imagination. When you finish, share your group's composition with the class.

Composition A

A Dangerous Driver

My friend Otto drives dangerously. For example, last week _____
_____
_____
_____
_____

Another time when Otto was giving me a ride to work, _____
_____
_____
_____
_____

The most frightening example of Otto's dangerous driving happened a few days ago. _____

_____

_____

_____

The next time I go somewhere with Otto, I'll offer to drive.

Composition B

My Messy Cousin

My cousin Fanny is the messiest person I know. I discovered this when she came to visit our family for a week last month. To give an example of her messiness, one day after she had made a sandwich for herself in the kitchen, I walked in and found _____

_____

_____

As another example of her messiness, on Saturday when she got back from shopping, she _____

_____

_____

The clearest example of the problem happened in the bathroom. Every day she

_____

_____

_____

Someone needs to teach Fanny to be neater when she stays as a guest in someone else's house.

Your turn 〜

Check the body of your composition to be sure there are plenty of specific details to support each example. Where can you add more details?

F Write a conclusion

THE CONCLUSION

When writing a conclusion for a composition that contains examples, you can end by writing a general statement that is true for all the examples and gives your feelings or opinions about them all. This ties the entire composition together and gives closure.

A conclusion can give closure to a composition in several different ways.

- A restatement of the main idea

  . . . It is good to live in a society that protects the freedom of the individual to have pets. However, the freedom to own dangerous pets must be limited in order to protect our freedom to live in a safe environment.

- A related idea that grows out of the composition

  . . . Even though these examples seem like minor incidents, all together they made me uneasy until I realized that I was experiencing a normal case of culture shock.

  . . . Now I can laugh when I tell these stories about my mother, but I sure wish her memory would improve a little.

- A look to the future

  . . . Well, I've had enough, so from now on I will let my answering machine pick up phone calls.

Practice 5

Write a conclusion for each of the following compositions.

Composition A

My Supportive Family

My family supports my decision to go back to school in the evenings. Everyone helps and contributes in some way. For example, my husband takes me to school and picks me up because parking is terrible. Besides, he doesn't want me walking alone in the parking lot at night. Also, my children help by taking turns doing the dinner dishes, since I don't have time in the evenings anymore. Even my sister helps out. Since she received her college degree last year, she has encouraged me and given me advice when I have papers to do.

_____

_____

Composition B

My Noisy Neighbors

My happy, peaceful world ended six months ago when my new neighbors moved in. They make a lot of noise. For example, they have loud parties three or four times a week. During these parties they play loud rock music, and the guests shout to each other above the music. All this noise continues until early in the morning, and I can't sleep until the party's over. Next, they have three dogs that bark almost all the time. This really bothers me in the evening after I have been working and going to school all day. I want to rest after a long day, but I can't. All of this is bad enough, but worst of all for me is that the husband and wife fight a lot. When they start arguing, they scream at each other. Then their kids get scared and start crying. It's impossible for me to study or to even think during all this. _____

_____

_____

Adapted from a composition by Ni Ni Mar

Your turn

Write a clear conclusion for your composition.

G Put together the first draft

As you have worked your way through Section II, you have written all the pieces that you need for a short composition: the main idea, the body, and the conclusion. Put these pieces together to create the first draft of your composition. Then add a title.

A Practice revising

Practice 6

Revise and rewrite the following draft on a separate piece of paper. Add a main idea, one transition signal, and specific, supporting details for one example, and a conclusion.

My Bad Luck

To start out, last Sunday I was at the mall shopping for new shoes. I decided on a pair, and the clerk put the information into the cash register. When I got ready to write a check, I discovered that my last check was gone. I didn't have enough cash, either. I was so embarrassed.

When I went to the movies the following week, I couldn't find my car in the parking lot.

My last example of bad luck is my worst. Last Thursday morning, I got into a car accident. I woke up very late that morning, and I thought I might make it on time for my eight o'clock class if I hurried. What of all things happened on that day? My car wouldn't start. I don't know how many times I repeated, "Please, come on!" Once I got it started, I had to rush to be on time because I only had ten minutes to make it. I stepped on the accelerator very hard. Suddenly, with a big noise, my car crashed into the car in front of me. I didn't see that the driver in front of me had stopped.

B Benefit from peer feedback

Exchange drafts with a partner. Read your partner's draft and check it using the *Revision Checklist* below. At this point, do not check grammar. Then give your partner feedback.

REVISION CHECKLIST ☑

☐ 1 Does the draft have any places that are unclear?

☐ 2 Is the draft organized clearly, according to the outline form on page 62?

☐ 3 Does the draft have a complete main idea sentence and a clear conclusion?

☐ 4 Is each example introduced with a transition signal?

☐ 5 Are there sufficient specific, supporting details for each example?

C Make revision decisions

Using the *Revision Checklist*, decide on the changes you want to make. Mark the changes in your first draft.

D Write the second draft

Write the second draft of your composition.

IV EDITING YOUR WRITING

A Check spelling

PERSONAL SPELLING LIST

The most effective way to improve your spelling is to keep a personal spelling list. Every time you find a common or useful word that you have had difficulty spelling, write the correct spelling on your personal spelling list. Keep your spelling list with you as you write and revise, so that you can check and add words.

Personal Spelling List
studying
writing
written
inconvenience

Practice 7

Check the spelling of these words, which are often used as reporting verbs in direct quotations. (See the box *Direct Quotations* on page 53.) Rewrite any misspelled words. Check your answers with a partner.

1 said
2 ansered
3 explaned
4 asked
5 cryed
6 shouted
7 screemed
8 whispered

Your turn

Start your own personal spelling list on a separate piece of paper.

B Edit for subjects, verbs, and spelling

Practice 8

Edit the following draft for subjects, correct past tense verbs, and spelling. Use a caret (∧) to show where to add words. There are 4 subject errors, 10 past tense verb errors, and 7 spelling errors for you to find.

How Can He Forget That?

¹My Uncle Quang often forgets things. ²For example, two months ago, my *grandfather* ~~granfather~~ ask him to go to the post office to send a package to one of our relatives. ³Uncle Quang say he would do it, but when returned from the post office, he announce that he forgot to take the package with him. ⁴My grandfather very dissappointed.

⁵Another time, when Uncle Quang took me to a Vietnamese restaurant, his forgetfulness make me very embarrassed. ⁶While he was dressing at home, I asked him if he had money in his pants pocket. ⁷Asked him this because he usually forgets his wallet when he changes pants. ⁸After our meal at the restrant, Uncle Quang discovered that his wallet not in his pants after all. ⁹The waiter looked at us while Uncle Quang searched all his pockets. ¹⁰I want to disapear.

¹¹Another example of Uncle Quang's forgetfulness took place recently when my grandmother asked him to take the family to the airport. ¹²When everyone ready to go, couldn't remember where his keys are. ¹³In a rush, everyone looked everywhere in the house for the keys. ¹⁴Than my ant asked him, "Have checked your pocket?" ¹⁵That's exactly where they were! ¹⁶The sight of my uncle finding his keys in his pocket make us laugh. ¹⁷If anyone knows of a treatment for forgetfulnes, please let me no. ¹⁸Uncle Quang really needs one.

Adapted from a composition by Vu Dang

C Benefit from peer feedback

Meet with a partner and exchange drafts. Read your partner's draft, and check for errors in subjects, verbs, and spelling.

D Write the final draft

Write your final draft, making the changes you have noted on your second draft.

A Share your writing

WRITING TO A CLASSMATE

There are many ways to share your writing with a classmate. One way is to exchange compositions and then write a short composition to your partner. It should identify the topic of your classmate's composition, summarize its most important points, and include a personal response from you.

Read this sample composition written in response to "How Can He Forget That?" on the opposite page.

In "How Can He Forget That?" Vu Dang gives three examples of his Uncle Quang's forgetfulness. In all three examples, Uncle Quang's forgetfulness is harmless. Perhaps he has inconvenienced and embarrassed his family, but no one has gotten hurt. In fact, the situations Vu describes are almost funny. When I read Vu's words, I could imagine the family's love for Uncle Quang and their forgiveness of his minor faults.

Reading about Uncle Quang reminded me of my Aunt May. Ten years ago she began forgetting things, similar to the kinds of things Vu's Uncle Quang forgets. About five years ago, Aunt May's forgetfulness got worse. Often she would go for a walk in the neighborhood, get lost, and wander the streets. Out of concern, my cousin took his mother to the doctor, and the doctor told him that Aunt May probably has Alzheimer's disease.

Maybe Uncle Quang is forgetful by nature. On the other hand, maybe Uncle Quang has a medical problem. In any case, it might be worth a visit to a doctor for a medical evaluation.

Exchange compositions with a classmate. Read the composition and write a composition responding to it. Include the elements below in your composition.

- A statement to identify your partner's composition
- A summary of the most important ideas in your partner's composition
- A response to your partner's composition, including your ideas

B Check your progress

After you get your composition back from your instructor, complete the *Progress Check* below.

PROGRESS CHECK

Date: _____

Composition title: _____

Things I did well in this composition:

_____

_____

_____

Things I need to work on in my next composition:

_____

_____

_____

Look at your *Progress Check* on page 56 of Chapter 2. How did you improve your writing in this composition?

_____

_____

_____

Supplying Reasons

What's your favorite pastime? Why do you enjoy it? Why did you decide on a certain career? Why did a particular historical event happen? People are usually interested in understanding why things happen.

In this chapter, you will write a main idea that raises the question "Why?" in the mind of the reader. You will then write a composition that provides reasons and supporting details that answer the question.

A Read sample compositions

As you read the following compositions, find the three reasons in each composition that explain and support the main idea sentence. In the margin, number each reason 1–3.

Sample 1

The Joy of Reading

I really enjoy reading whenever I have free time. One reason I love to read is that I can visit other countries by reading about others' travel experiences. My favorite travel book tells about a trip to Africa. In it the author describes his adventures finding fascinating tribes, dense jungles, and the rarest animals in the world. In another travel book, the author writes about visiting interesting places in Europe and describes walking through Renaissance cathedrals in Italy, climbing the Eiffel Tower in Paris, and waking up to foggy mornings in London.

Another reason I love to read is that it puts me in a good mood. When I am disappointed about something, I can read a story about someone who overcame a similar disappointment. When I'm sad, I can read a funny story that makes me laugh. When I am discouraged, I can read about a person who helps others. The people I read about give me strength and hope.

The main reason that I enjoy reading is that it allows me to travel in time and space. I can travel to the Renaissance period and watch Michelangelo sculpt David. I can have dinner with King Louis XIV or Queen Victoria of England. I can move next door to Beethoven and listen to his music as he's composing it. I can also travel to Mars and Jupiter. It's really fun to visualize myself in the past and in the future.

I can't imagine life without the joy of reading.

Adapted from a composition by Heera Lee

Sample 2

The International Bridge

I go online as often as I can for the following reasons. First of all, I can shop on the Internet without leaving my room. On the other hand, if I go shopping in the stores, it takes me all day because I have to drive to several stores to find what I want at a reasonable price. When I shop on the Internet, it takes me only about a half hour to find what I want, compare prices, and order it. I can even shop online to buy things from other countries.

Second, I can send photos to people anywhere in the world in less than five minutes without leaving my home. If I mail photos using the postal service, however, I have to go out to get copies made of the photos. This takes a couple days and two trips. Then I have to take another trip to the post office to buy the right amount of postage. After I put the photos in the mail, it takes several days for them to arrive at their destination.

The most important reason for me to go online is to keep in touch with my friends and family. Calling overseas costs a lot of money. Luckily, I can stay in close contact with the people who are important to me when we communicate by e-mail. The best part of my day is the afternoon when I sit down at my computer to check my e-mail and pick up messages from home. I know, too, that my family really enjoys hearing from me often.

These days going online is an important part of my life. For me, it's an international bridge that connects me to any place I want in the world.

Adapted from a composition by Kamyar Amjadi

Preventing a Worldwide Disaster

The amounts of heat-trapping gases inside the Earth's atmosphere have been increasing since the beginning of the Industrial Revolution in the 17th century. The causes are many, but some of the most important include the following. First, methane gas results from several commercial activities, such as coal mining, the production of petroleum products, and the raising of cattle.

Next, the cutting down and burning of forests contributes to the increase of carbon dioxide in the atmosphere. When wood burns, carbon dioxide is released. The burning of forests, then, produces billions of tons of carbon dioxide each year. In addition, the cutting down of forests takes away trees that would normally remove carbon dioxide from the air.

Another source of increasing carbon dioxide in the Earth's atmosphere is the burning of fossil fuels. A primary example of fossil fuels is the gasoline we burn in our vehicles. The use of fossil fuels has added enormous amounts of this gas into the atmosphere. In the late 20th century, the burning of fossil fuels released about six tons of carbon dioxide each year. Figures for the 21st century are certain to be much higher. The result of these increasing amounts of heat-trapping gases in our environment is a serious threat to the health of our planet Earth. We must act immediately in order to prevent a worldwide disaster.

Napoleon's Fall from Power

In early 19th century Europe, the French leader Napoleon Bonaparte fell from power for the following reasons. First, he became more and more self-centered. Because of his egotism, he refused to accept valuable suggestions from his advisors. He believed that he was born to rule all of Europe, and that no one could stop him.

Second, Napoleon's Continental System caused more damage to France and its friends than to its enemies. Napoleon tried to prevent British products from entering the continent, but the countries within the continent needed many of these products. France suffered without these products and supplies.

Finally, Napoleon's aggressive military caused the people to turn against him. It became obvious to them that Napoleon's goal was to treat the people unfairly and become a king with total control over all. In addition, too many Frenchmen were dying. This situation led to many personal, military, and economic difficulties. Thus, a man who many believed in at first ended up losing the confidence of the people and falling from power. Lonely and defeated, Napoleon Bonaparte died in 1821.

B Select a topic

Read the following topics to select one for your composition. Choose a topic that brings to mind several reasons. Also, make sure that you can provide plenty of specific, supporting details for the reasons.

1 The reasons for an important decision you have made, such as moving to another country or city, getting married, or choosing a particular major or career

2 The reasons you enjoy a particular hobby

3 The reasons you enjoyed or did not enjoy a specific trip or vacation

4 The reasons you made a major purchase, such as a computer or car

5 The reasons you like or dislike a particular store, restaurant, or place of entertainment

6 The reasons for a specific problem in the 21st century

7 The reasons for a specific historical event or situation

8 Other topics: _____

C Explore ideas by making a list

LISTING AND ORGANIZING IDEAS

Making a list of your ideas is a good way to explore a topic. When you make a list, allow your mind to explore. Write everything that comes to mind as you did for the freewriting technique in Chapter 3 on page 61. You don't have to write complete sentences. Afterward, you can analyze your list and put related groups of ideas together.

Here are the steps to explore a topic.
1 Make a list of ideas about your topic.
2 Decide on a main idea that most of the ideas on your list support.
3 Cross out ideas that do not relate to your main idea.
4 Group relevant ideas together.
5 Write a general statement that is true for each group of supporting ideas.

Practice 1

Look at this page from a student's notebook, which shows a student exploring a topic by making and organizing a list. The student has completed the first three steps in the box *Listing and Organizing Ideas* on page 79. Work with a partner and complete steps 4 and 5. Group the ideas together into three reasons and write a general statement for each group of ideas that support that reason. The first general statement is written for you.

Barking all the time, jumping on people, knocking things over
Washing the dog regularly, getting rid of fleas in its fur
~~*Dogs are good company – can play with them and have fun*~~
It costs a lot to feed a dog.
~~*Feeling safe and protected by a large dog at home, in the night*~~
What if the dog bites people, hurts children?
If I go away on vacation, I will have to pay to put the dog somewhere or pay for a dog sitter.
Cleaning up after the dog – Yuck!
~~*Good exercise – taking the dog for a walk*~~
I like sleeping late on the weekends and don't want to have to wake up early to take the dog out.
~~*Can meet other people who have dogs*~~
What about medical bills if the dog gets sick – that can be very expensive.

1 *Dogs can be dangerous and difficult to control.*
2 __________
3 __________

Your turn

For your topic, brainstorm a list of ideas. Following the steps in the box *Listing and Organizing Ideas* on page 79, organize your ideas and write three reason statements to support the main idea about your topic.

II PREPARING THE FIRST DRAFT

A Make a rough outline

Using notes from the list you brainstormed on the opposite page, make an outline similar to the one on the right. Then complete it, writing key words, phrases, and ideas.

I. MAIN IDEA
II. BODY REASON 1 Details REASON 2 Details REASON 3 Details
III. CONCLUSION

B Compose the main idea

THE MAIN IDEA

A clear main idea sentence includes a topic and a comment. In a composition supplying reasons, the comment gives the writer's opinion about the topic.

Topic: Reading
Comment: I enjoy it whenever I have free time.
Main idea: I enjoy reading whenever I have free time.

Practice 2

In each of the following pairs of sentences, one gives a main idea, and the other gives supporting details or reasons. Circle the letter of the main idea in each pair.

1 a Soccer gives me a chance to be with my friends.
   b My favorite hobby is soccer.

2 a My decision to leave home was one of the hardest decisions I've ever had to make.
   b My little brother cried when he heard I was thinking about moving out on my own.

3 a I love living in an apartment alone.
   b I can keep my apartment as messy as I want.

4 a Communicating in a second language can cause misunderstandings.
   b Living in a foreign country can be difficult.

5 a A college education should be every teenager's goal.
  b Without a college education, it is hard to find a career that pays a good salary.

6 a The Metropolitan Museum in New York is a wonderful place to visit.
  b The museum has a large collection of high quality paintings.

7 a It costs a lot to own a dog.
  b Owning a dog causes many problems.

Your turn ↶

Look back at your rough outline and write your main idea sentence.

C Organize reasons in a logical order

ORGANIZING REASONS

Because the reader usually remembers the last point most clearly, the most common way to organize a composition that contains reasons is to put the most important or most convincing reason last. When you look at your notes before starting to write your first draft, you should think about which reason is the most important and contains the most convincing details. That reason should be the final one in your composition.

Practice 3

Read the following composition, and answer the questions on the next page.

Why I Gave Up Smoking

After three years of trying to quit smoking, I finally gave up the habit six months ago for several good reasons.

To begin with, I got tired of the smell. My hair usually smelled bad, I always had bad breath, and my apartment always smelled like cigarette smoke.

Second, I felt uncomfortable when people reacted negatively to my smoking. Complete strangers would give me unfriendly looks and move away from me. Even my girlfriend began to avoid me.

Next, cigarettes just kept getting more and more expensive. I estimate that smoking cost me over one hundred dollars a month.

The most important reason, though, is that I began to worry about my future health. I do not mind having a little cough, but I am really afraid of health problems when I get older, such as cancer and heart disease. No pleasure is worth that price! Now that I have quit smoking, I can enjoy clean air again, people are friendly toward me, I have more spending money, and my cough is gone. Life is just more enjoyable.

---

1 What are the writer's four reasons for giving up smoking?

2 Which one is the most important reason? Why?

Your turn ↶

Organize the points for your composition in logical order. Mark the order in your outline. In most cases, your most important, strongest, or most convincing reason will appear last.

D Use transition signals to introduce reasons

TRANSITION SIGNALS

Transition signals can indicate the introduction of a reason. These expressions help your reader follow your ideas from one reason to the next.

The first reason is that . . .
Another reason is that . . .
The most important reason is that . . .

First of all, . . .
Second, . . .
Finally, . . .

Practice 4

Write the transition signals used in each of the sample compositions at the beginning of this chapter (pages 76–78).

1 Sample 1, "The Joy of Reading"

_____   _____   _____

2 Sample 2, "The International Bridge"

_____   _____   _____

3 Sample 3, "Preventing a Worldwide Disaster"

_____   _____   _____

4 Sample 4, "Napoleon's Fall from Power"

_____   _____   _____

Practice 5

Add transition signals to the following composition.

My Neighbors

Lately, I have been miserable because of the neighbors who moved next to my house in April. _____ they do
(1)

not control their dogs. I used to have a nice garden with beautiful flowers, and I could not understand why the flowers were disappearing. One day I woke up from the barking of the dogs, looked out the window, and saw the dogs jumping around in my garden.

_____ is that they have wild
(2)

parties. Almost every evening they have people over. They must have many relatives and friends. They turn the music up so loud that it almost kills my ears. Then they start shouting and dancing.

_____ is that almost every night
(3)

after midnight they start fighting. A week ago someone called the police because they started yelling and arguing in front of their house. Before these people moved in, my neighborhood was nice and quiet. I hope they move away and leave the neighborhood the way it used to be.

Adapted from a composition by Tiopa Techiryan

Your turn ↶

Decide on transition signals for your composition and note them on your outline.

E Use specific, supporting details

SUPPORTING DETAILS

Specific details and facts can be used to support reasons. Details may relate to the five senses: sight, sound, touch, smell, and taste.

Sight: I used to have a nice garden with beautiful flowers.
Sound: I woke up from the barking of dogs.
Touch: Some dogs have very soft fur.
Smell: My apartment always smelled like cigarette smoke.
Taste: The freshly baked bread was delicious.

Practice 6

In pairs or small groups, use your imagination to write details to support the reasons in the following composition.

Dining Disaster

I'll never eat at Rosco's Steak House again. First of all, the service is terrible.

_____

_____

_____

_____

Another reason I'll never go back is that the atmosphere is unpleasant.

_____

_____

_____

_____

What convinced me more than anything else, though, was the food.

_____

_____

_____

_____

I don't understand how a place like Rosco's can stay in business.

Your turn ↲

Check your outline for specific details, and add more details to support each reason. Then write the body of your composition, using your outline and notes.

F Write a conclusion

THE CONCLUSION

In a composition supplying reasons, the conclusion may restate the main idea to give closure.

. . . I can't imagine life without the joy of reading.

. . . These days going online is an important part of my life. For me, it's an international bridge that connects me to any place I want in the world.

. . . The result of these increasing amounts of heat-trapping gases in our environment is a serious threat to the health of our planet Earth. We must act immediately in order to prevent a worldwide disaster.

Practice 7

Write a conclusion for the following composition.

Paris: My Dream Come True

Ten years ago, after years of dreaming about Paris, I finally got to take the trip of my dreams. There are several reasons why this trip was so memorable. First of all, the hotel location was fantastic. It overlooked the Seine, the famous river I had read about in so many poems. In the morning, my husband and I had delicious café au lait and sweet-smelling, warm croissants for breakfast. We listened to the laughter of children playing nearby and watched the river go by below. It ran by very slowly and gave me the feeling that it was telling me the long story of Paris.

Next, Montmartre was wonderful. This is where many painters gather. When we went up the hill, we saw lots of artists from all over the world painting on their canvases. The air was filled with the sounds of happy people and the smell of paint.

What I enjoyed most, though, were the cafés. One of my dreams was just to have a cup of coffee at a café in Paris. I had seen so many pictures of those cafés in books, and finally, my dream came true. I really enjoyed watching people walking on the street and listening to them speak French. Some of them wore gorgeous dresses. Some of them were casual. But everyone had a sense of style.

_____

_____

_____

Adapted from a composition by Teruyo Tsuchiya

Your turn

Write a conclusion for your composition.

G Put together the first draft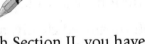

As you have worked your way through Section II, you have written all the pieces that you need for a short composition: the main idea, the body, and the conclusion. Put these pieces together to create the first draft of your composition. Then add a title.

III REVISING YOUR WRITING

A Practice revising

Practice 8

Revise and rewrite the following composition. For each reason, make sure there is a transition signal and there are specific, supporting details. Move details from one location to another so that they support the appropriate reason.

No More Big City for Many People

It is no surprise that every year many people move out of the big cities in this country. One reason that they move is that they are unhappy about the air quality.

Next, they get tired of the traffic and crowds. Smog covers most big cities like a large umbrella.

Also, many people are tired of the high crime rate related to drugs, car thefts, murders, and riots. The crime rate keeps going up, and no one feels safe in big cities anymore.

---

continued

Lots of people move out because they cannot find housing at a reasonable price. Young couples cannot afford to buy their own homes in large cities. Students face the toughest hardships of all because of their limited incomes. Because of this, they often have to live with many roommates or with relatives. It is unfortunate that so many people are forced to leave a city that they may think of as their home.

B Benefit from peer feedback

Exchange drafts with a partner. Read your partner's draft and check it using the *Revision Checklist* below. At this point, do not check grammar. Then give your partner feedback.

REVISION CHECKLIST ☑

☐ 1 Does the draft have any places that are unclear?

☐ 2 Is the draft organized clearly, according to the outline form on page 81?

☐ 3 Does each reason begin with a transition signal?

☐ 4 Is each reason supported by plenty of specific details?

C Make revision decisions

Using the *Revision Checklist,* decide on the changes you want to make. Mark the changes in your first draft.

D Write the second draft

Write the second draft of your composition.

IV

EDITING YOUR WRITING

A Identify clauses

> ### INDEPENDENT AND DEPENDENT CLAUSES
>
> All sentences must have at least one *independent clause.* An independent clause has at least one subject and one verb. An independent clause expresses a complete thought and can stand alone as a sentence.
>
>   S   V
> Zahib plays the cello.
>
> A *dependent clause* cannot stand alone as a sentence because it does not express a complete thought. It depends on an independent clause to complete its meaning. A subordinating conjunction usually introduces a dependent clause.
>
> Common subordinating conjunctions
>
> **Time:**   before, after, when, while, as soon as, just as, until, whenever
> **Contrast:**   although, even though, though
> **Condition:**   if, unless
> **Cause/Effect:** because, since
>
>   S   V
> After Zahib gets his undergraduate degree in music, he will get a job.
>
>   S   V   +   V
> Because Zahib studies hard and gets good grades, he won a scholarship.

Practice 9

Label each clause as independent (*I*) or dependent (*D*). If a clause is independent, add a period at the end.

_____ **1** I go online

_____ **2** As often as I can

_____ **3** I can shop on the Internet without leaving my room

_____ **4** If I go shopping in the stores to buy something

_____ **5** It takes me all day

_____ **6** Because I have to drive to several stores to find what I want at a reasonable price

_____ **7** When I shop on the Internet

_____ **8** It takes me only about a half hour to find what I want

_____ **9** Since I can shop online to buy things from other countries

_____ **10** These days going online is an important part of my life

B Identify sentence types

Practice 10

Edit the following groups of sentences by combining two of the sentences into a compound or complex sentence. Add coordinating or subordinating conjunctions, if needed. Also, make any necessary changes in punctuation and capitalization.

My Precious Harmonica

1 I love to play my harmonica. Whenever I can.

2 One reason is that it relaxes me. It is easy to carry. I can take my harmonica to school.

3 I can put it in my book bag. I don't have to do homework between classes. I can play it in the car for a few minutes and feel relaxed.

4 Next, the harmonica is so easy to play. I hear a new song on the radio. I can pick up my harmonica and play the tune right away.

5 The most important reason I like my harmonica so much is that when I see or touch it, I can feel my father's love. He gave me a shiny, new harmonica as a birthday present ten years ago. He often enjoyed my playing.

6 Playing my harmonica reminds me of my father. I play it. I can see his face and hear his voice.

7 I thank my father for introducing me to this wonderful hobby. It is something I can pass on to my own son some day.

Adapted from a composition by Jee Moon

C Benefit from peer feedback

Exchange drafts with a partner. Read your partner's draft and check for a variety of sentence types: simple, compound, and complex. Make sure one sentence type isn't overused.

D Write the final draft

As you write your final draft, check for a variety of sentence types: simple, compound, and complex. Make improvements, as needed. Also, check for grammar errors.

V FOLLOWING UP

A Share your writing

Before you turn in your final draft, do one of these activities to share your writing.

1 Small Group Read-Around (page 35)
2 Traveling Compositions (page 55)
3 Writing to a Classmate (page 73)

B Check your progress

After you get your composition back from your instructor, complete the *Progress Check* below.

PROGRESS CHECK

Date: _____

Composition title: _____

Things I did well in this composition:

_____

_____

_____

Things I need to work on in my next composition:

_____

_____

_____

Look at your *Progress Checks* in the previous chapters. How did you improve your writing in this composition?

_____

_____

_____

Supporting with Parallel Points

What are your goals for the future? What do you miss about a place where you used to live? Who are your favorite musicians? What are the advantages (or disadvantages) of technology in the 21st century?

In the composition for this chapter, you will provide three parallel points to support your main idea. *Parallel* means belonging to the same category, such as three goals, three things you miss, three ways of doing something, or three advantages of something.

A Read sample compositions

Read the following compositions. Have you had thoughts or opinions similar to those expressed by the writers? Discuss your answer with a partner.

Sample 1

Homesick for Indonesia

The three things I miss about Indonesia are the parties, my social status, and my family. Thinking about the parties in my native country really makes me homesick. When people have a party, they give an open invitation for everyone in the neighborhood to attend. Guests spend long hours talking, relaxing, and laughing.

The next thing that I miss is the social status I used to have. I used to be a manager in a computer training company. When I decided to move to this country, I had to give up my position and the status that went with it. I miss the respect I used to get from my customers, the company instructors, and my students.

The thing I miss the most about my country is my family, especially when I think about the family birthdays we celebrated almost every month. Most of all, I have been very lonely here without my wife. I have tried to fill my time with studies and sports, but nothing stops me from thinking about her constantly, especially in the loneliness of midnight. If I were a bird, I would fly to meet her.

Writing about what I miss helps me get over my homesickness for a short time, but it never goes away completely.

Adapted from a composition by Sofjan Hendrata

Sample 2

My Three Main Goals

I have three main goals for the next five years. First of all, I want to finish my education. In the past, I was a student at the University of Guadalajara for a year. I loved the university atmosphere because it gave me a sense of purpose. Presently, I enjoy being back on a college campus. Even though taking English classes slows me down a little, I am committed to my goal of getting a degree in accounting.

Next, after I become an accountant, I will be in a better position to support my children in their education. As a professional, I'll make a better salary and will be able afford the expenses of college for my children. Also, I will be an example for my kids of someone who attends college to learn and grow.

My last main goal is to keep my family together. I have seen families fall apart because everyone becomes so involved in their own lives that they forget about the others in their family. My dream for my family is that after my kids get married, we can still live together in the same building. Perhaps we'll be able to buy a four-unit apartment building, where we can all live together, as several separate families that belong to one big family. I look forward to achieving all these goals so that my family can be successful and stay together as one big, happy family.

Adapted from a composition by Manuel Garcia

Sample 3

High Renaissance Artists

Three of the most well-known artists of the Italian High Renaissance (16th century) include Leonardo da Vinci, Rafael, and Michelangelo. Da Vinci's *Mona Lisa* is perhaps the world's most famous portrait. People throughout the years have been fascinated with the subject's beautiful and mysterious smile.

continued

Another High Renaissance painter is Rafael. Most people consider Rafael's *Madonna with the Goldfinch* to be the most graceful and dignified painting of the subject matter ever produced. Rafael also painted extraordinary murals. Many appear on the walls of famous churches in Rome.

Like Rafael, Michelangelo is also famous for the murals he painted. Most people are familiar with his beautiful paintings on the ceiling of the Sistine Chapel. The artist also created extraordinary statues. One of the finest examples of Michelangelo's statues is the impressive thirteen and a half foot tall *David* in Florence.

These three masters of the High Renaissance inspired many artists that followed them. They have also left much beauty for us to enjoy in the 21st century.

Sample 4

Reducing Greenhouse Gases

Scientists warn that we need to reduce unwanted greenhouse gases in our environment, especially carbon dioxide. We can do so in various ways. First, we must reduce the carbon dioxide we allow into the environment. We can do this by changing from coal and oil to cleaner fuels. Coal-burning electric plants produce large quantities of carbon dioxide. On the other hand, burning natural gas produces fifty percent less carbon dioxide than coal. The best sources of electricity, however, include water, wind, and solar power.

Another important way to cut the amounts of carbon dioxide we put into the environment is by burning less fuel for heating and transportation. We can add insulation materials inside the walls of buildings and install windows that conserve heat. As for cars, we need to replace vehicles that get poor gas mileage with ones that get much better mileage. A good example of a car with excellent gas mileage is the hybrid car. A hybrid, which is gas- and electric-powered, gets up to 50 miles per gallon in the city.

Last, some experts have recommended a "carbon use tax" to encourage people, manufacturers, and electricity companies to reduce their use of fossil fuels such as coal and oil. Coal would be taxed the most because it contains the most carbon. This tax would also encourage engineers and scientists to develop substitutes for gasoline fuel.

If we want to protect our environment, we need to take immediate and strong actions. We must reduce the greenhouse gases that are destroying the Earth as we know it.

B Select a topic

> **TOPICS**
>
> When you select a topic, choose one that you can develop with specific, supporting details. For some topics, you may want to do some research on the Internet or at the library.

Select a topic from the list below. In your composition you will need to include reasons and examples with specific, supporting details.

1 Your goals for the future

2 What you miss or don't miss about a place where you used to live

3 Things that you particularly like or don't like about life in the 21st century

4 The benefits or drawbacks of computers, cell phones, cars, television, or some other piece of technology that we use every day.

5 Solutions to a specific concern in the 21st century

6 Other topics: _____

C Explore ideas

Do one of these activities to explore your topic.

1 Freewrite about your topic, writing down everything that comes to mind.

2 List ideas about your topic and group them into categories.

II PREPARING THE FIRST DRAFT

A Make a rough outline

To plan your first draft, make an outline similar to the one on the right. Then complete it, writing key words, phrases, and ideas.

I. MAIN IDEA
II. BODY POINT 1 Details POINT 2 Details POINT 3 Details
III. CONCLUSION

B Compose the main idea

THE MAIN IDEA

A clear main idea sentence includes a topic and a comment. In a composition with parallel points, sometimes the comment lists the points.

Topic: Indonesia

Comment: I miss the parties, my social status, and my family.

Main idea: The three things I miss about Indonesia are the parties, my social status, and my family.

An alternative is to give an opinion in the comment.

Topic: The greenhouse gases in our environment

Comment: Scientists warn that we need to reduce them, especially carbon dioxide.

Main idea: Scientists warn that we need to reduce unwanted greenhouse gases in our environment, especially carbon dioxide.

Look at the main idea of sample composition 2 on page 95. What type of comment is used: list of points or opinion? What type of comment is used in sample composition 3?

Practice 1

Write main ideas for these topics.

1 Hobbies

_____

2 Goals

_____

3 A specific area of technology

_____

4 Artists, musicians, or musical groups

_____

5 World peace

_____

Your turn ↝

Write the main idea for your composition.

C Organize your points

> ### ORGANIZING POINTS
>
> Here are two common ways to organize points in a composition.
> - Time order   Organized according to when things occurred
> - Order of importance   Organized with the most important point last

Practice 2

Identify the method of organization in these compositions.

1 Sample 1, "Homesick for Indonesia" (pages 94–95)

_____

2 Sample 2, "My Three Main Goals" (page 95)

_____

Your turn ↲

With a partner or in a small group, take turns telling about your topic. Follow these steps.

1 Tell what your main idea is and why you chose it.
2 Give your three points and explain them in some detail.
3 Ask if your points and details clearly support your main idea and if they are in a good order.

D Use transition signals to introduce points

> ### TRANSITION SIGNALS
>
> In some compositions with parallel points, there may not be a transition signal for the first point.
>
> Point 1   (No transition signal.)
> Point 2   The next thing that I miss is . . .
> Point 3   The thing I miss the most is . . .

Practice 3

Write the transition signals used in the sample compositions at the beginning of this chapter.

1 Sample 1, "Homesick for Indonesia"

_____   _____   _____

2 Sample 2, "My Three Main Goals"

_____   _____   _____

3 Sample 3, "High Renaissance Masters"

_____   _____   _____

4 Sample 4, "Reducing Greenhouse Gases"

_____   _____   _____

Practice 4

Add transition signals to the following composition.

My Goals for the Future

I have three main goals. _____
(1)
is to open my own day care business. Right now I'm a babysitter in my home,
but I want to open a location outside my home. Once I get set up, I want to
take care of children up to the age of three. I really love this stage of childhood.

_____ is to speak and write
(2)
English very well. This is important to me because I've chosen to live in the
United States, where English is spoken. If I want to be successful in my day
care business and feel more comfortable talking with people, I have to speak
English better than I do now.

_____ is the one I hold closest
(3)
to my heart. I want to be married and have children. Ever since I was a child,
family was the most important thing in my life. Now as an adult, I would like
to have my own family and my own children. Of course, I also want to have a
good husband to share my life joys and sorrows with. I hope that I can achieve
these three very important goals for my future.

Adapted from a composition by Teresa Poteranska

E Write points to introduce details

SUPPORTING A POINT

Usually a point is followed by details that support it.

Point:

The most disturbing annoyance for me is the large amount of junk mail that I receive.

Details:

Every day my mailbox is completely filled with mostly useless material. I hate to go through all the junk to separate out what's important from what's not. Some junk mail appears to be very important or official. For a person like me who cannot read English very well, it is very confusing and time-consuming.

Practice 5

Write the missing points for the following composition. Include transition signals, and write complete sentences.

My Three Main Goals

I have three main goals. _____
_____ Several of my friends have college degrees, and they tell me that if I want a better future, I need to work hard and get a degree. I don't want to be like one of my neighbors who has been looking for a job for several months. She is not qualified for anything more than a minimum wage position.

_____

After I get my degree, I want to look for a new job or ask for a promotion in my present job. Eventually, I'll earn more money and be able to afford to buy my own house.

_____

I met a person from Spain a year ago, and he told me about a lot of interesting historical places to visit, such as the Alhambra, Toledo, and the Museo del Prado. Also, I want to experience first hand the living culture and customs. Maybe I'll even go to the running of the bulls in Pamplona. I'm picturing myself in the crowds in Pamplona watching the bulls running down the street, with the spectators shouting and cheering. In five years, I plan to have a degree, a better job, a house, and a round-trip ticket to Spain in my hand.

Adapted from a composition by Claudia Ortiz

Your turn ↶

Write three clear points for your composition.

1 _____

2 _____

3 _____

F Use specific, supporting details

Practice 6

Form a small group of three to four students. Together, complete the following composition by adding specific details to support the points.

My Three Hobbies

I have three enjoyable hobbies. To begin, I love surfing the Internet.

_____

_____

_____

Next, I really enjoy shopping at _____

_____

_____

_____

My favorite hobby is playing _____

_____

_____

_____

Your turn ↶

Write the body of your composition. Make sure that you have plenty of specific details to support each point.

G Write a conclusion

Practice 7

Write conclusions for the following compositions. You may wish to review the box *The Conclusion* on page 68.

Composition A

The Benefits of Community Colleges

In the United States, attending a two-year community college before transferring to a four-year university offers several advantages. First, community colleges are generally more numerous than universities. This means that most people can find a community college closer to home than they can a university. The convenience of being closer to home saves on the cost of transportation and housing.

Second, the cost of fees or tuition is usually much lower at a community college than it is at a university. It's not uncommon that a student will have to pay at least five times the amount to attend a university than a community college. Community colleges are definitely easier on a person's budget.

Because of the cost advantage, students are freer to explore subject areas that might interest them. With this flexibility to explore, students may find new areas of interest and decide on a career they hadn't previously considered. _____

_____

_____

Composition B

Homesick for Eritrea

Even though I like my freedom in the United States, I still get homesick for my native country, Eritrea. I especially miss the Red Sea coast, the wedding customs, and my family.

I often think about the Red Sea coast. Every weekend my family and I would go to Masawa on the coast. It was so pleasant to sit in the warm sun on the sand and watch my family and the other people swimming and having a good

continued

time. Also, I could spend time in the naturally heated steam baths. I would feel relaxed and refreshed afterwards.

In addition to missing the family outings on the Red Sea coast, I also miss the wedding celebrations of my people. The hosts of a wedding invite all friends and neighbors to attend the event. The party lasts all day and night, with traditional food, drink, and dancing. Everyone has a delightful time.

Most of all, though, I miss my mother. She was a big help to me. Every day while I was working she took care of my family. After I finished work and returned home, my mother and children were waiting for me with smiles on their faces and delicious food on the table. Then we sat down together to enjoy a wonderful meal and pleasant conversation. After the children were in bed, my mother and I enjoyed chatting for a while. I miss hearing about her past experiences and getting her advice about things that are on my mind.

_____

_____

Adapted from a composition by Nigisty Ghebre

Your turn

Write a conclusion for your composition. Use one of the following conclusion types.
- A restatement of the main idea
- A summary of the points
- A related idea that grows out of the body
- A look to the future

H Put together the first draft

As you have worked your way through Section II, you have written all the pieces that you need for a short composition: the main idea, the body, and the conclusion. Put these pieces together to create the first draft of your composition. Then add a title.

A Practice revising

> ### REVISING
>
> When you revise, you should check for these elements in your composition.
> - A clear, complete main idea sentence
> - Transition signals
> - Clear parallel points
> - Specific, supporting details for each point
> - A conclusion that gives closure

Practice 8

Check the following composition for each of the elements listed above. Then revise and rewrite it on a separate piece of paper.

Time Takers

The first one is that every time I make a business telephone call, it takes a long time to find the information I need. Often, I have to try several times because I keep getting a busy signal. When I finally do get through, I just hear a recorded menu, and it takes a long time to listen to the choices, since there are so many. After making my way though all of that, often I find out that the message or person does not have the information I need. Or, I may be put on hold again for quite a while. It's a big waste of time.

Every day it takes me about ten minutes to gather all the dirty clothes because the kids throw them everywhere. Sometimes I have to wash a couple of loads a day, so often I spend one or two hours a day washing, folding, and ironing clothes. I wish someone would invent a machine that could wash and iron the clothes all at once.

Last, I spend a lot of time cleaning my house. Normally, it takes an hour to clean a room, but the kids' bedroom and the kitchen take me even longer.

Adapted from a composition by Maria Lucero Mora

B Benefit from peer feedback

Exchange drafts with a partner. Read your partner's draft, and check it using the *Revision Checklist* below. At this point, do not check grammar. Then give your partner feedback.

REVISION CHECKLIST ☑

☐ 1 Does the draft have any places that are unclear?

☐ 2 Is the draft organized clearly, according to the outline form on page 97? Is the most important or most recent point last?

☐ 3 Does the draft have a complete main idea sentence?

☐ 4 Are transition signals used to introduce points?

☐ 5 Are there plenty of specific, supporting details?

☐ 6 Is there a conclusion that ties the entire composition together?

C Make revision decisions

Using the checklist above, decide on the changes you want to make. Mark the changes in your draft.

D Write the second draft

Write the second draft of your composition.

IV EDITING YOUR WRITING

A Edit for run-on sentences

RUN-ON SENTENCES

A run-on sentence is a common error. It consists of two (or more) independent clauses that are not joined correctly.

Here are the most common types of run-on sentences.

- Two independent clauses with only a comma between them

  I like to be ready for emergencies, I always take my cell phone with me.

- Two independent clauses with no punctuation between them

  I finished shopping at Sports Barn I discovered that my keys were locked in the car.

  My brother came right away with the extra key my cell phone is so handy.

There are several ways to correct a run-on sentence.

- Add a coordinating conjunction (*and, but, so*) to make a compound sentence.

  I like to be ready for emergencies, so I always take my cell phone with me.

- Add a subordinating conjunction (*when, since, if*) to make a complex sentence.

  When I finished shopping at Sports Barn, I discovered that my keys were locked in the car.

- Separate the two independent clauses to make simple sentences.

  My brother came right away with the extra key. My cell phone is so handy!

Practice 9

Underline the 8 run-on sentences in the following composition.

My Stressful Life

¹Three things give me a lot of stress: traveling long distances by plane, worrying about being late for an appointment or school, and taking tests. ²Long plane flights make me very nervous. ³I can't stand being seated for hours at a time, especially in a small, confined space. ⁴Worst of all is sitting in a window seat next to someone I don't know who is sleeping, I feel trapped.

⁵Next, being late for class stresses me out if, for example, I wake up late for school, I get really panicky and start rushing. ⁶Sometimes I drive too fast because I worry about parking. ⁷If it takes too long to find parking, I run to the classroom, when I get to class, I'm out of breath and sweating. ⁸The worst parts about being late are thinking I've missed something important and knowing that I'm disturbing the class. ⁹Being late is like a nightmare for me, I do everything I can to avoid being late.

¹⁰Last, tests make me very anxious. ¹¹My stress doesn't mean that I haven't studied, it means that I'm nervous about not completing the test on time and not answering all the questions perfectly. ¹²Sometimes my mind goes blank even if I really know the answers. ¹³If it's a writing test, I worry about not having any good ideas. ¹⁴I would be happy if I never had to take another test in my life, I think this is a common problem for students.

¹⁵In conclusion, most of my stress is related to school, I go to school four days a week, I take long flights only occasionally. ¹⁶However, I choose to go to school I choose to take trips. ¹⁷The truth is that the benefits and pleasure I get from school and trips make the stress worth it.

Adapted from a composition by Farzaneh Sheroke

Practice 10

With a partner, rewrite the 8 run-on sentences from *Practice 9*.

B Edit for stringy sentences

> **STRINGY SENTENCES**
>
> Stringy sentences are sentences that are too long. They are too long because they have too many independent clauses joined together with coordinating conjunctions such as *and, but,* or *so.*
>
> Stringy
>
> > In Egyptian classrooms, when students address teachers, they must do so very carefully, so they must never interrupt, and they must use very polite forms of speech when they talk to a teacher.
>
> Correct
>
> > In Egyptian classrooms, when students address teachers, they must do so very carefully. They must never interrupt, and they must use very polite forms of speech when they talk to a teacher.

Practice 11

Mark the stringy sentences in the following composition by drawing a line in the right margin. Write *STR* to the right of the line. The first sentence is marked for you. Then discuss with your class ways to rewrite the stringy sentences correctly.

The Worrisome Side Effects of Computers

¹Computers have several bad side effects that worry me. ²One negative side effect is that people can get addicted to computers. ³Their addiction forces them to spend all their free time in front of the computer, so this obsession damages family life because these people no longer spend enough time with their loved ones, and people can rely too much on computers to do their work, so when the computer is down for some reason, these people become distressed.   *STR*

⁴Another bad side effect is that using a computer for many hours can be harmful to a person's health. ⁵Back problems and wrist pain are common for people with computer jobs, and computers can cause eyestrain, which can lead to headaches, and people who work with computers for long periods of time can become overweight from the lack of physical activity, but getting physical therapy can minimize these problems.

---

⁶The most worrisome side effects are those associated with children. ⁷There are parts of the Internet that children should not see. ⁸Some Internet chat rooms are one example. ⁹Signing on to a chat room can be dangerous for children because they are inexperienced, and adults can easily trick them, and newspapers have reported several cases of children being taken advantage of by adults after visiting a chat room. ¹⁰Another aspect of the Internet that could be harmful for children is advertising or Web sites that advertise adult products or even unsafe items such as power tools.

¹¹Perhaps limits would provide the solution. ¹²If people could limit their time on the computer, they might avoid becoming addicted and having other health problems. ¹³Even more important, if children were not allowed on a computer without their parent's presence, they could be protected from material for adults only.

Adapted from a composition by Farzaneh Sheroke

C Write the final draft

As you write your final draft, make the revisions and edits you have noted on your second draft. Check for run-on sentences and stringy sentences.

V FOLLOWING UP

A Share your writing

Before you turn in your final draft, do one of these activities to share your writing.

1 Small Group Read-Around (page 35)
2 Traveling Compositions (page 55)
3 Writing to a Classmate (page 73)

B Check your progress

After you get your composition back from your instructor, complete the *Progress Check* below.

PROGRESS CHECK

Date: _____

Composition title: _____

Things I did well in this composition:

_____

_____

_____

Things I need to work on in my next composition:

_____

_____

_____

Look at your *Progress Checks* from the previous chapters. How did you improve your writing in this composition?

_____

_____

_____

Interpreting Quotations and Proverbs

Can you think of any common proverbs from your native language? Can you think of any well-known quotations? Proverbs and quotations are usually short statements that contain a great deal of wisdom. Do you have any favorites that say what you think about life?

In this chapter, you will write about a proverb or quotation. You will interpret its meaning, give your personal opinion about it, and then develop your opinion with points and specific, supporting details.

A Read sample compositions

The following compositions each have two main parts. The first part interprets the meaning of a quotation or proverb. The second part gives a response that explains and supports the writer's opinion. Read each composition. Draw a line to indicate where the second part starts.

Sample 1

An Exception

The saying "When in Rome, do as the Romans do" (St. Ambrose) means that wherever a person goes, he should follow the habits of the people who live there. Often this is true, but there are exceptions. For example, when I came to this country, I didn't know very much about U.S. customs. I did know one custom, though. I knew that Americans keep their shoes on in the house.

One day I was invited to the house of my father's American friend. It was the time for me to use my only knowledge about Americans' habits. As soon as the door opened and I took my first step to enter the house, I felt strange because I entered the house with my shoes on. Soon after that, my father's friend said very politely, "Could you please take off your shoes?" I was surprised, but soon I understood. My father's friend was wearing slippers inside the house. Quickly, I took off my shoes and changed into slippers.

When we were having dinner, I told my father's friend that I thought Americans wore shoes in their house. He told me that he had lived in Japan for several years and that he liked the Japanese way of wearing slippers in the house. So, he had adopted the Japanese custom. From this experience I learned that doing "as the Romans do" is good advice most of the time, but we must also be ready for any exceptions.

Adapted from a composition by Takejiro Hirayama

Sample 2

You Can't Judge a Book by Its Cover

The saying "You can't judge a book by its cover" means that you should not judge any person because of his or her appearance or your first impression of that person. For me, this saying is true, based on a personal experience that changed my life.

Two years ago when I visited my brother in Jordan, I met his roommate. At first sight I didn't like him because he looked shy and unexciting. Later, I asked my brother, "Are you happy with your roommate?" He replied, "Yes, I'm lucky to have a roommate like him." I was surprised and asked why. My brother then told me great stories about his roommate. For example, at an early age, he led prayers, and everyone honored him for his good character. Also, he was only sixteen when he went to college and by the time he was twenty-two, he had his master's degree.

The more I got to know my brother's roommate, the more I came to respect him. I found that he was intelligent, kind, honest, and sincere in his dedication to all that is noble and good. The unexpected outcome is, if you haven't already guessed, that this "shy and unexciting" person is my husband now, and we are very happy together. This experience taught me that a person can't judge a book by its cover.

Adapted from a composition by Lobna Kara-Ali

Sample 3

A Spanish Proverb for Drivers

The Spanish proverb *"Es mejor perder un minuto en la vida, que la vida en un minuto"* means that it is better for a person to lose a minute of his or her life than to lose life in one minute. This wise saying is advice for people who are in a hurry and drive too fast. To illustrate, I saw a terrible accident once when the driver of a truck was driving too fast.

continued

My mother and I were getting a ride home to Ayacucho in the back of a truck. The driver of another truck behind us was in a big hurry and driving very fast. It started to rain, and our truck slowed down, but the other truck passed us and disappeared up ahead. About a dozen people were riding in the open back of the truck.

After about a half an hour, we arrived at a bridge. Something was wrong. Our driver stopped, and we got out to see what was going on. As I looked ahead, I could see a truck lying upside down in the river. For a moment, I didn't realize which truck it was. Then I saw that it was the truck that had passed us not long ago. The people who had been riding in the back were now trapped underneath. I felt sick to my stomach when I realized that my mother and I could easily have chosen to return home in the truck that had gone off the bridge.

Fortunately for us, we chose to ride in the truck with the driver who decided that it was not worth trying to get home fast in the rain.

Adapted from a composition by Jeanette Blake

Sample 4

Haste Makes Waste

The English proverb "Haste makes waste" means that people often lose time in doing something rapidly and carelessly. As an example, last summer I went hiking with two friends. When they got ahead of me on the hiking trail, I took a different but more difficult trail to save time. I tried to go faster but then I took a bad step and fell, twisting my ankle. For the rest of the hike, I had to go very slowly on my injured foot. In trying to save time, I ended up wasting time.

Another example took place recently when I was making myself a cup of coffee in the morning. I was rushing because I needed to get to school early for an appointment. My elbow hit the edge of the coffee container, which fell off the counter and onto the floor, spilling the coffee all over the floor. I lost precious time cleaning it all up.

One more example happened last weekend when I bought a new exercise bicycle. The bicycle came in a box, and I had to put it together. I was excited to try out my new bicycle as soon as possible, so I quickly took the parts out of the box and set the instructions aside. Then I assembled the parts without reading the instructions. Unfortunately, I missed some important steps, and the bicycle didn't work correctly. As a result, I had to take the bicycle apart, read the instructions, and try again. Now it works properly, and I'm sorry I wasted my time hurrying to put it together.

I know now that when I hurry and do things too quickly, I usually end up wasting time. Based on these experiences, whenever I want to hurry in the future I'm going to remind myself that "Haste makes waste." Then, I'll take the time I need.

By Thuong Phung and Ann Strauch

B Select a topic

Read the following proverbs and quotations. Then choose one to write about, either from the ones below or one that you know. Select one that you have a clear opinion about and that you can develop with specific, supporting details.

Proverbs

1 "A friend in need is a friend indeed." (United States)
2 "Where there's a will there's a way." (United States)
3 "The world belongs to the whole world." (Japan)
4 "You cannot buy a friend with money." (Russia)
5 Other proverb: _____

Quotations

1 "The weak can never forgive. Forgiveness is the attribute of the strong." (Mahatma Gandhi, Indian leader)
2 "You must do the thing you think you cannot do." (Eleanor Roosevelt, former first lady of the United States)
3 "Ask not what your country can do for you; ask what you can do for your country." (John F. Kennedy, President of the United States, 1961–1963)
4 "No man is an island." (John Donne, 17th century English author)
5 Other quotation: _____

C Explore ideas by clustering

Look at the student idea cluster on the next page about the proverb "Haste makes waste." Then follow these steps to create an idea cluster for your topic.

1 In the center of a sheet of paper, write the proverb or quotation you chose, and draw a circle around it. Next, come up with ideas and write them around your chosen proverb or quotation. Circle each idea, and draw a line to connect it with the proverb or quotation.

2 Continue to add ideas, connecting each new idea with another. In this way, one idea will lead to another, and you will end up with a page of ideas that branch out from the proverb or quotation.

3 After you have produced a full page of ideas, select one branch or several related branches to write about.

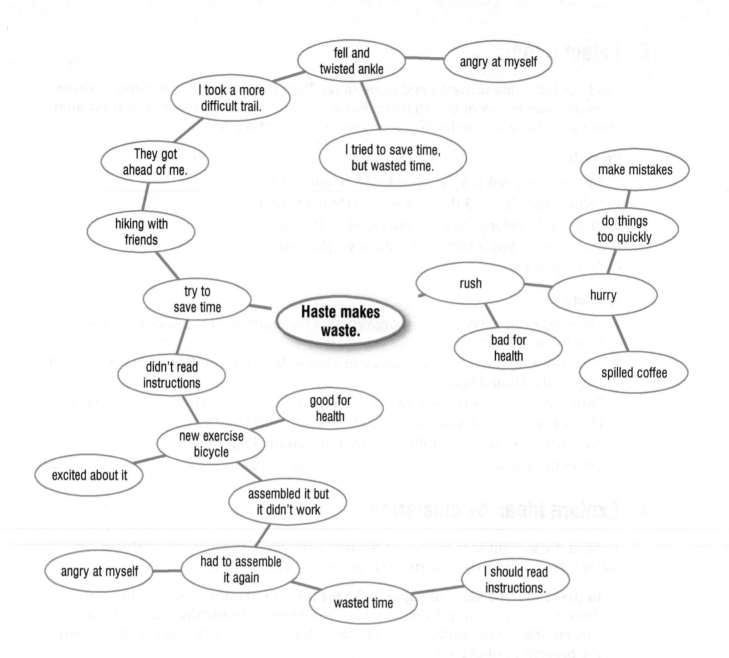

D Discuss your ideas with others

In a small group, follow these steps to tell about your proverb or quotation.

1 Tell what your proverb or quotation is and why you chose it.

2 Explain your idea cluster, and the ideas you have chosen to write about.

II PREPARING THE FIRST DRAFT

A Make a rough outline

Using ideas from your cluster, make an outline similar to the one on the right. Then complete it, writing key words, phrases, and ideas.

I. MAIN IDEA
Quoted proverb or quotation
Author or source
Meaning
II. BODY
Support for your opinion
III. CONCLUSION

B Compose the main idea

THE MAIN IDEA

A clear main idea sentence includes a topic and a comment. When interpreting a proverb or quotation, the comment can state its meaning.

Topic: The saying "You can't judge a book by its cover"

Comment: You should not judge any person because of his or her appearance or your first impression of that person.

Main idea: The saying "You can't judge a book by its cover" means that you should not judge any person because of his or her appearance or your first impression of that person.

Practice 1

With a partner or in a small group, write a main idea for each topic.

1 "Don't count your chickens before they hatch." (Proverb)

The proverb "Don't count your chickens before they hatch" means that a person can't be too certain about what will happen in the future.

2 "Mistakes are part of the dues one pays for a full life." (Sophia Loren)

_____

_____

3 "Two heads are better than one." (United States)

_____

_____

4 "Keep your face to the sunshine and you cannot see the shadow." (Helen Keller)

_____

_____

5 "United we stand; divided we fall." (Kentucky state motto) .

_____

_____

6 "Animals are such agreeable friends; they ask no questions, pass no criticisms." (George Eliot)

_____

_____

Your turn ↲

Write the main idea for your composition.

C Organize the body

> **ORGANIZATION**
>
> Organize the body in a way that fits the support you are providing. There are several possible methods of organization.
> - One extended example (narration)
> - Several examples or reasons
> - Other parallel points (points belonging to the same category)

Practice 2

For each of the compositions at the beginning of this chapter, identify the method of organization: extended example or several examples.

1 Sample 1, "An Exception" _Extended example_ _____

2 Sample 2, "You Can't Judge a Book by Its Cover" _____

3 Sample 3, "A Spanish Proverb for Drivers" _____

4 Sample 4, "Haste Makes Waste" _____

Your turn ↲

Review your outline and decide what kind of organization you will use in your composition.

D Use sense details for description

Practice 3

Successful writers often use sense details to make the scene they are describing come alive for the reader. The following examples are from a composition. Read each example and underline the sense details. The first one is done for you.

1 *Sight:* The moon <u>lit up</u> nature and turned it into a <u>beautiful oil painting</u>.

2 *Sound:* Nature played a romantic song to me with the humming of insects and the wind in the bushes.

3 *Smell:* The breeze brought to my nose the smell of the rice field behind my house.

4 *Taste:* My tongue could even taste salt on my lips, salt brought from the sea by the gentle breeze.

5 *Touch:* Then the cold wind would chill me and gently push me back into the warmth of my house.

Practice 4

Read the following composition and identify the sense details. Underline the sense details and write the corresponding senses – sight, sound, smell, taste, and touch – in the right margin.

Warmth in the Winter

[1]"He is happiest, be he king or peasant, who finds peace in his home" by Goethe means that home can be the happiest place of all. [2]I felt an especially close personal bond to my family's <u>warm</u> house in the <u>snowy</u> wintertime *feeling, sight* during school vacations. [3]It was located at the edge of a hilly forest near a big lake in the heart of Europe. [4]After I had skated for a full day with my junior hockey team, the evening fell very fast. [5]Shadows began to fall on the lake, and the air suddenly became as cold as the ice we skated on. [6]The warmth of home called to me just a walk away through the snowy fields.

[7]When I opened the front door to my house, the smells from my mother's cooking immediately surrounded me. [8]I entered into a comfortable square living room, well protected from the cold, windy weather outside. [9]A soft light glowed in the corner. [10]My first step into this loving interior gave me a magical feeling. [11]After I changed into thick socks and slippers, I sat down to a large bowl of spicy, hot soup that my dear mother had prepared for my

---

continued

return. [12]After I ate, I joined my father on the couch, where he read a book to me, discussed my hockey games, and exchanged jokes with me. [13]My father's calm, deep voice and the warmth of his love filled my tired body.

[14]I did not realize then how lucky I was. [15]In later years, though, I came to understand how safe and peaceful my childhood had been in that warm and cozy house in Czechoslovakia.

Adapted from a composition by Bob Krupka

Practice 5

Work in a small group. Complete the following composition by writing specific, supporting details for each of the points.

Kinship in Nature

"One touch of nature makes the whole world kin" by Shakespeare means that when we enjoy nature, we become closer to all our human brothers and sisters. To illustrate, last summer my wife and I visited a beautiful sandy beach. When we arrived, the sun was just starting to set. The beach _____
_____
_____

A family with two children approached us, and _____
_____
_____

A similar experience took place when we took a picnic to the park last month. I brought my soccer ball, and _____
_____
_____

More recently, just yesterday when I was sitting under a tree on campus and feeding bread to a squirrel, a few other students started tossing popcorn our way. _____
_____

It was amazing to me how these three experiences in nature gave me an instant sense of kinship with total strangers. Without a doubt, Shakespeare was right about how nature reminds us that all people are brothers and sisters.

Your turn ～

Write the body of your draft, using clear organization and appropriate sense details.

E Write a conclusion

THE CONCLUSION

The conclusion ties the entire composition together and reminds the reader of your main idea.

> Because of this experience, I completely agree with the proverb *"Es mejor perder un minuto en la vida, que la vida en un minuto."* (It is better for a person to lose a minute of his or her life than to lose life in one minute.) This wisdom saved my life that day, and it could save my life again. It's just not worth risking lives in order to save a little time.

Practice 6

Write a conclusion for the following composition.

A Successful Spirit

"If wrinkles must be written upon our brows, let them not be written upon the heart. The spirit should not grow old." This quotation by James A. Garfield means that even in old age, people are capable of great things. To give an example, the great Italian artist Michelangelo was 71 years old when he painted the Sistine Chapel. As another example, the physician and humanitarian Albert Schweitzer was still performing surgery in his African hospital at the age of 89. Finally, painter Grandma Moses didn't start painting until she was 80 years old. After that, she completed over 1,500 paintings. _____

_____

_____

Your turn ～

Write a conclusion for your composition.

F Put together the first draft

In this section, you have written all the pieces that you need for a short composition: the main idea, the body, and the conclusion. Put these pieces together to create the first draft of your composition. Then add a title.

A Check for wordiness

> ### WORDINESS
>
> *Wordiness* means the use of too many words to express an idea. One solution to wordiness is to rewrite the wordy sentence, taking out the unnecessary words. The revised sentence will be shorter and much clearer.
>
> Look at how this sentence was revised for wordiness.
>
> Original version
>
> "One man's meat is another man's poison" is an English proverb from years ago that means that sometimes something may be right in one way or another for one person, but wrong for another person in some way that we may notice, but not always, obviously depending on the situation.
>
> Revised version
>
> "One man's meat is another man's poison" is an old English proverb that means that something might be right for one person but wrong for another person.

Practice 7

Revise these wordy sentences. They are a continuation of the composition about the proverb "One man's meat is another man's poison."

1 I agree for the most part or almost entirely and most of the time with this proverb.

_____

2 Almost nothing that I can think of right now can be right or good or wonderful or favorable for everyone in the world.

_____

3 For example, I love classical music, but my husband loves jazz when he's in any kind of mood to listen to music.

_____

4 When I listen to classical music, I can relax and feel rested and happy at any time.

_____

5 When my husband listens to jazz, he feels energetic and awake, not sleepy or lazy anymore.

_____

6 As another example, I absolutely love and really enjoy a lot going on hikes in any suitable location.

_____

7 On the other hand, unlike me, my husband prefers and would rather go cycling on his bicycle to any suitable location.

___

8 We don't have exactly the same preferences that the other has, but we have learned to work together and compromise instead of holding on to our own preferences no matter what.

___

Your turn ✏

Check your composition for wordiness. Revise sentences as needed.

B Benefit from peer feedback

Exchange drafts with a partner. Read your partner's draft and check it using the *Revision Checklist* below. At this point, do not check grammar. Then give your partner feedback.

REVISION CHECKLIST ☑

☐ **1** Does the draft have any places that are unclear?

☐ **2** Is the draft organized clearly, using an extended example, several examples, reasons, or other parallel points?

☐ **3** In the opinion section, does the draft provide enough specific, supporting details? Can any sense details be added?

☐ **4** Is the draft free from wordiness?

C Make revision decisions

Using the *Revision Checklist*, decide on the changes you want to make. Mark the changes in your draft.

D Write the second draft

Write the second draft of your composition.

IV

EDITING YOUR WRITING

A Edit for correct use of articles

ARTICLES WITH COUNT NOUNS

Use the articles *a, an,* and *the* (or other determiner) before a singular count noun.

a book, a truck, a bridge, a cup of coffee, a personal experience

an example, an experience, an accident

the box, the proverb, the edge, the darkness

Practice 8

Check these sentences for the correct use of the articles *a* and *an*. Mark what should be inserted.

1 "Long sentences in ʌ*a* short composition are like large rooms in ʌ*a* little house." (Shenstone)

2 "Never answer letter when you are angry." (Chinese proverb)

3 "Every man is poet when he is in love." (Plato)

4 "After the rain, there's no need for umbrella." (Bulgarian proverb)

5 "There can be no rainbow without cloud and storm." (J. H. Vincent)

6 "If you kick stone because you are angry at it, it will only hurt your foot." (Korean proverb)

7 "Friend's frown is better than fool's smile." (Hebrew proverb)

8 "One finger cannot lift pebble." (Iranian proverb)

NONCOUNT NOUNS

Do not use *the* before a noncount noun when the noun is being used in a general statement.

Incorrect	Correct
The music calms the soul.	Music calms the soul.
The honesty is the best policy.	Honesty is the best policy.
The love cures all.	Love cures all.

Practice 9

Check the following sentences for the correct use of the article *the*. Mark what should be deleted or inserted. Not all sentences contain errors.

1 "Even <u>the</u> lion has to defend himself against flies." (German proverb)

2 "Mind grows by what it feeds on." (J. G. Holland)

3 "The music should strike fire from heart of a man, and bring tears to the eyes of a woman." (Beethoven)

4 "Anger is a bad advisor." (Hungarian proverb)

5 "The necessity is the mother of the invention." (Proverb)

6 "The curiosity killed the cat." (American proverb)

INDEFINITE AND DEFINITE ARTICLES

The indefinite article *a* is commonly used before the first mention of a singular count noun.

> I was watching <u>a man</u> cross the street when suddenly <u>a fire engine</u> came screaming through the intersection . . .

However, in later uses of the same noun, the definite article *the* is normally used because the reference has become definite, or known.

> . . . <u>The man</u> jumped onto the curb to avoid <u>the fire engine</u>.

Practice 10

Fill in the blanks with the articles *a*, *an*, or *the*.

1 Last winter my husband and I took _____ (1) hike to _____ (2) beautiful remote beach. We didn't expect to run into anyone on _____ (3) beach, but we did. In the distance we could see _____ (4) family approaching, and when they got near, we started talking. Their small son saw _____ (5) sand crab, and soon we all became fascinated with _____ (6) sand crab. We felt like old friends.

2 Not long ago, my girlfriend and I went hiking in Griffith Park. We stopped for lunch under _____ (1) large, shady tree. As we sat under _____ (2) tree, we noticed _____ (3) beautiful, blue bird nearby. _____ (4) bird was looking for food. My girlfriend tossed _____ (5) piece of bread to it, but _____ (6) bread rolled back toward us. _____ (7) bird hesitated for a moment but then quickly grabbed _____ (8) piece of bread and flew away with it. In a few seconds, three more birds appeared, all loudly asking for food.

3 Last summer, my family and I visited _____ beautiful canyon. When we got out
(1)

of our car to look into _____ canyon, I saw _____ snake nearby. I shouted for my
(2)   (3)

parents to come and look, but when they came, _____ snake was gone. My father
(4)

made a joke about it, but I didn't appreciate _____ joke. I'm afraid of snakes!
(5)

DEFINITE ARTICLES IN SPECIFIC CONTEXTS

In certain contexts, some nouns take the definite article.

- In the context of a person's house

    the door, the floor, the kitchen counter, the edge of the counter

- In the context of the public environment

    the bank, the post office, the mail carrier, the library, the street

- In the context of nature

    the moon, the sun, the beach, the desert, the stars

A definite article is used before a count noun when the noun is followed by
specific information that modifies it.

    Last night I visited <u>an</u> unusual house.

    Last night I visited <u>the</u> unusual house <u>of my father's friend</u>.

    Today I learned <u>an</u> English proverb.

    Today I learned <u>the</u> English proverb <u>"Haste makes waste."</u>

Practice **11**

Edit the following for the correct use of the article *the*.

Ahhh, Nature!

¹When I was a child, my mother often told me, "Nature takes the cares of
the world away." ²I didn't understand that at the time, but now I do. ³I'm glad I
remembered her wisdom yesterday. ⁴After the alarm rang in the morning, I went
down to kitchen to make myself of a cup of coffee. ⁵I put a jar of instant coffee
on counter. ⁶Then by accident I hit jar with my hand, and it fell onto floor,
spilling coffee everywhere.

⁷After I got dressed, I left house and went to library to get a book, but book
I wanted was already checked out. ⁸Then I went to post office to get some
stamps. ⁹Line was too long, so I left. ¹⁰After that, I went to a cash machine for
some money, but it was out of service.

> ¹¹Upset, I decided to go to beach to relax for a while. ¹²It was a beautiful day. ¹³Sky was blue with puffy, white clouds, and sun was shining brightly. ¹⁴I could even see moon faintly on horizon. ¹⁵A breeze was blowing softly. ¹⁶Instantly, I felt calm and at one with nature. ¹⁷I no longer cared about my worries.

B Benefit from peer feedback

Meet with a partner and exchange drafts. Read your partner's draft, and check for the correct use of articles. Discuss any possible errors.

C Write the final draft

As you write your final draft, edit your composition for articles, other grammar errors, and spelling errors. As a reminder, if you use the spell checker on your computer, be careful to select the correct word for the context.

V FOLLOWING UP

A Share your writing

Before you turn in your final draft, do one of these activities to share your writing.

1 Small Group Read-Around (page 35)
2 Traveling Compositions (page 55)
3 Writing to a Classmate (page 73)

B Check your progress

After you get your composition back from your instructor, complete the *Progress Check* below.

PROGRESS CHECK

Date: _____

Composition title: _____

Things I did well in this composition:

_____

_____

_____

Things I need to work on in my next composition:

_____

_____

_____

Look at your *Progress Check* on page 110 of Chapter 5. How did you improve your writing in this composition?

_____

_____

_____

Writing a Summary

Have you ever explained to a friend what happened in a movie you saw or in a story you read? Have you ever summarized for a friend the most important ideas in a magazine article or a textbook chapter you read?

In this chapter, you will read a selection and write a short summary of it.

A Read a story and a newspaper article

Read the following story and newspaper article. After you read the two selections, work with a partner and discuss the following questions for each piece.

1 What is the main idea?
2 What are the most important details?
3 What are the least important details?

Selection 1

One at a Time

A friend of ours was walking down a deserted Mexican beach at sunset. As he walked along, he began to see another man in the distance. As he grew nearer, he noticed that the local native kept leaning down, picking something up, and throwing it out into the water. Time and again he kept hurling* things out into the ocean.

As our friend approached even closer, he noticed that the man was picking up starfish that had been washed up on the beach and, one at a time, he was throwing them back into the water.

Our friend was puzzled. He approached the man and said, "Good evening, friend. I was wondering what you are doing."

"I'm throwing these starfish back into the ocean. You see, it's low tide right now, and all of these starfish have been washed up onto the shore. If I don't throw them back into the sea, they'll die up here."

"I understand," my friend replied, "but there must be thousands of starfish on this beach. You can't possibly get to all of them. There are simply too many. And don't you realize this is probably happening on hundreds of beaches all up and down this coast? Can't you see that you can't possibly make a difference?"

The local native smiled, bent down and picked up yet another starfish, and as he threw it back into the sea, he replied, "Made a difference to that one!"

(From Chicken Soup for the Soul *by Jack Canfield and Mark V. Hansen)*

hurling: *throwing with great force*

Selection 2

Why Mona Lisa Smiles

Women, as a rule, smile more than men, but the difference between the sexes disappears depending on the circumstances. For women, smiling is the default option.* For men, the default is not smiling.

"If you don't know what to do – and you're a female – you smile because you know you're not making a mistake. If you're a man, you don't smile," says Marianne LaFrance, a psychology professor at Yale University.

In the largest analysis of smile studies ever done, LaFrance and her colleagues evaluated research involving nearly 110,000 people, finding many variations in smiling behavior.

For example, they found differences when people thought they were being observed and when they thought they were alone. When observed, women smiled more than men. When not being scrutinized,* there was little difference between the sexes.

"That suggests that people behave according to what they believe is appropriate," says LaFrance, the lead author of the study. According to some researchers, smiling is less a sign of underlying* emotion than a social display meant for others.

Put a woman in front of a mirror or a shop window, though, and even alone, she's more likely to smile. "We're practicing what we're supposed to be doing most of the time. We just want to make sure," says LaFrance.

Differences in smiling all but disappear, reports LaFrance, when men and women were in the same occupation or social role. "In care-taking roles – as a therapist or nurse, for instance – differences were nonexistent."

If you want to bet on who smiles most, put your money on the white, teenage girl who is with someone she doesn't know – she's no doubt in default mode. Smiling differences between the sexes become larger during the teen years.

continued

"The comprehensiveness of this analysis is outstanding," says Dacher Keltner, a psychology professor at University of California at Berkeley and director of the Berkeley Center for the Development of Peace and Well-being. "There are studies of people smiling in social contexts, by themselves, in different cultures and at different ages." The study was published in the March 2003 issue of *Psychological Bulletin.*

*(Adapted from "Why Mona Lisa Smiles" by Dianne Partie Lange,
the* Los Angeles Times, *April 14, 2003)*

default option: *what is normal or automatic, especially in computer settings*
scrutinized: *examined carefully*
underlying: *the real cause or reason for something*

B Analyze summaries

Practice 1

Read the following summaries of "One at a Time" and "Why Mona Lisa Smiles." Discuss the questions below with a partner.

1 What information did the summary writers include in the first sentence?
2 Were the details they chose to include the same as the ones that you said were the most important?
3 Find several details in the selections that were not mentioned in the summaries. Why were these details not included?

Summary 1

Summary of "One at a Time"

"One at a Time" by Jack Canfield and Mark V. Hansen, from their book *Chicken Soup for the Soul,* tells the story of a man who wants to make the world a better place. The man is on a beach in Mexico and is throwing starfish back into the ocean to save their lives. A second man approaches him. The second man says that there are too many starfish to toss back, so throwing only some of them back won't make any difference. As the first man tosses another starfish back into the water, he makes the point that it has made a difference to the one he has just tossed back.

Summary 2

Summary of "Why Mona Lisa Smiles"

In the *Los Angeles Times* article "Why Mona Lisa Smiles" by Dianne Partie Lange (April 14, 2003), the author reports on the findings of Marianne LaFrance. LaFrance is a psychology professor at Yale University who analyzed smile studies. She found that, in general, women smile more than men. When women and men are watched, women smile more than men. This difference between men and women is the greatest in the teen years. Teenage girls smile much more than teenage boys. On the other hand, the differences between men and women are less in certain situations. When women and men are not watched, the differences between them disappear. The differences also disappear for men and women in the same occupation or social role.

C Select a topic

Select a topic to summarize from the list below.

1 An article from a newspaper or a magazine
2 A short story or a folktale
3 An excerpt from a novel or a textbook
4 The following folktale, "Cornelia's Jewels"

Cornelia's Jewels
A Folktale

The sun was shining brightly on a glorious morning in ancient Rome. Two boys were standing in a beautiful garden. They were looking at their mother and her friend, who were walking among the flowers and trees.

"Have you ever seen a more attractive lady than our mother's friend?" asked the younger boy, holding his tall brother's hand. "She looks like a queen."

"She's pretty, but she's not as elegant as our mother," answered the older boy. "She has rich clothing and shiny hair, but her face is not honest and kind. It's our mother who looks like a queen."

"You're right," said the other. "No woman in Rome can match our dear mother for her beauty and queenliness."

Soon, Cornelia, their mother, came down the path to speak with them. She was simply dressed in a plain white robe. Her arms and feet were bare, as this was the custom in those days. And she wore no rings on her fingers or sparkling necklaces around her neck. The only crown she wore consisted of her soft brown hair. A sweet smile lit up her noble face as she looked into her sons' proud eyes.

"My sons," she said, "I have something to tell you."

continued

They bowed to her, as Roman children were taught to do, and said, "What is it, Mother?"

"I'd like for you to have dinner with us in the garden. Our friend is going to show us that wonderful chest of precious jewels that we have all heard so much about."

The brothers looked shyly at their mother's friend. How could it be possible for her to have more jewels than the ones she wore? On her hands she had six rings with huge jewels, and around her neck, there were at least five chains of gold with jewels.

When the simple meal was over, a servant brought the chest out from the house. The lady opened it. It was filled with chains of gold, shining and glistening; ropes of pearls, as white as milk and as smooth as satin; heaps of rubies, as red as glowing coals; sapphires, as blue as the summer sky; emeralds, as green as new summer grass; and diamonds, flashing and sparkling like rays of the sun.

The brothers looked at the jewels for a long time.

"Oh," whispered the younger boy. "If only our dear mother could have such beautiful things!" The older boy stood silent.

Finally, the lady closed the chest, and the servant took it away.

"Is it true, Cornelia, that you don't have any jewels?" asked the mother's friend. "You have no gold, no rubies, no pearls, no sapphires, no emeralds, no diamonds? Is it true, as I have heard people whisper, that you are poor?"

"No, I am not poor," answered Cornelia. As she spoke she gently pulled her sons to her side. "Here are my treasures. They are worth much more than all your gold and jewels."

D Explore ideas by listing

LISTING IMPORTANT POINTS

Making a list of important points will help you prepare to write a summary about an article or story. After you have listed points, eliminate any unnecessary ones.

Practice 2

Look at the list of points about the story "One at a Time" by Jack Canfield and Mark V. Hansen. Draw a line through any unnecessary points.

1 A man is on a beach in Mexico.

2 He's throwing live starfish back into the ocean.

3 It's a deserted Mexican beach at sunset.

4 It's low tide.

5 The man keeps tossing them out into the ocean.

6 He doesn't want them to die on the beach.

7 A second man approaches him.

8 The second man says that there are too many starfish to toss back.

9 Throwing only some of them back won't make any difference.

10 The first man tosses another starfish back into the water.

11 He makes the point that it has made a difference to the one he has just tossed back.

Your turn ↜

Write a list of the most important points about the selection you chose as your topic in *Select a topic* on page 133. Then cross out any unnecessary details.

Topic: _____

E Discuss your ideas with others

With a partner or in a small group, discuss your list. Can you delete any more unnecessary details? Can you add any additional points?

II PREPARING THE FIRST DRAFT

A Make a rough outline

Use the information from your list to make an outline similar to the one on the right.

SUMMARY
Main idea

Body

B Compose the main idea

THE MAIN IDEA

In a summary, a clear main idea sentence includes the title, the author or source, and the main idea of the selection. The title of an article or story is in quotation marks. The name of a book, magazine, or newspaper is underlined. When a paper is typewritten, sometimes *italics* are used instead of underlining.

Title:	"Why Mona Lisa Smiles"
Author:	Dianne Partie Lange
Source:	Los Angeles Times, April 14, 2003
General idea:	The author reports on the findings of Marianne LaFrance
Main idea for summary:	In the Los Angeles Times article "Why Mona Lisa Smiles" by Dianne Partie Lange (April 14, 2003), the author reports on the findings of Marianne LaFrance.

Practice 3

With a partner, write a main idea for a movie with which you are both familiar. Start your main idea sentence by giving the name of the movie and either the name of the director or of one of the stars.

> *In the movie . . . , starring . . .*
> *In the movie . . . , directed by . . .*

Movie title: _____

Stars/director: _____

Main idea: _____

_____

_____

_____

Your turn

Write the main idea for your summary.

C Summarize essential ideas

> ### SUMMARIZING
>
> The body of a summary briefly explains the original selection. When you write the body, follow these guidelines.
> - The summary body should be much shorter than the selection.
> - Use your own words. If you quote exact phrases or sentences from the original, use quotation marks.
> - Include all of the essential ideas.
> - Leave out unnecessary details.

Practice 4

Look back at the sample compositions at the beginning of Chapter 6 on pages 112–114. On a separate piece of paper, write several sentences to briefly summarize one of the compositions.

D Put together the first draft

You have written the main idea for your summary paragraph. To finish, write the essential ideas for the body of your paragraph.

III REVISING YOUR WRITING

A Delete unnecessary details

> ### REVISING
>
> Usually it is important to include specific, supporting details in the body of a composition (for example, in a narration composition). On the other hand, for the body of a summary, you only need to include the most important points. Thus, when you revise a summary, look for and delete unnecessary details.

Practice 5

Cross out the 5 sentences with unnecessary details in the summary below.

> ### Summary of "How Much Land Does a Man Need?"
>
> ¹"How Much Land Does a Man Need?" by Leo Tolstoy is a short story about the tragic consequences of greed. ²Peter begins as a poor farmer. ³He acquires more land and becomes a rich man, but he's not happy. ⁴He still wants more land. ⁵He then travels to a place where the people sell their land cheaply, according to their tradition. ⁶According to the ways of these people, for a cheap price, Peter can buy whatever amount of land he can walk around in one day. ⁷Unfortunately, Peter tries to walk much too far because he wants to claim a large amount of land. ⁸He starts at 5:00 in the morning and walks very quickly to cover as much land as possible. ⁹He notices that the land is very beautiful, flat, and fertile. ¹⁰Peter thinks about where he can plant fruit trees and where he can plant potatoes. ¹¹The temperature is at least 90 degrees Fahrenheit. ¹²Peter's mouth is dry, and his water bottle is empty. ¹³He barely makes it back to the starting place, where he dies of complete exhaustion.

B Benefit from peer feedback

Exchange drafts with a partner. Read your partner's summary and check it using the *Revision Checklist* below. Then give your partner feedback.

REVISION CHECKLIST ☑

- ☐ 1 Does the draft have any places that are unclear?
- ☐ 2 Is the draft organized clearly, according to the outline form on page 135?
- ☐ 3 Does the draft have any unnecessary details?

C Make revision decisions

Using the *Revision Checklist,* decide on the changes you want to make. Mark the changes in your first draft.

D Write the second draft

Write the second draft of your summary.

IV EDITING YOUR WRITING

A Edit for verb tense

THE LITERARY PRESENT

When you summarize fiction, you explain the main points of the story using present tense verb forms. In a summary, the *literary present* is used even if story is written in the past tense or the author is no longer alive.

Compare the excerpt from the story "One at a Time" and a sentence from the summary.

Excerpt

". . . As our friend approached even closer, he noticed that the man was picking up starfish that had been washed up on the beach and, one at a time, he was throwing them back into the water."

Summary

The man <u>is</u> on a beach in Mexico and <u>is throwing</u> starfish back into the ocean to save their lives.

Practice 6

Edit the following summary for correct use of the literary present. There are 5 errors.

¹"Key Item" by Isaac Asimov is a short science-fiction story about a team of scientists trying to find out why a computer is not working. ²Because this is an important computer, it had to be fixed soon, but nobody could come up with the solution. ³After the scientists argue about it for a while, one of them figured out the problem. ⁴The computer wanted the scientists to include "please" in their commands to it. ⁵Once they say "please," the computer started working perfectly.

B Benefit from peer feedback

Meet with a partner and exchange drafts. Read your partner's draft and check for verb tense errors.

C Write the final draft

As you write your final draft, make the revisions and edits you have noted. Write the title at the top of the page following the style in the sample summaries on pages 132–133.

V

FOLLOWING UP

A Share your writing

Before you turn in your final draft, do one of these activities to share your writings.

1 Small Group Read-Around (page 35)
2 Traveling Compositions (page 55)
3 Writing to a Classmate (page 73)

B Check your progress

After you get your composition back from your instructor, complete the *Progress Check* below.

PROGRESS CHECK

Date: _____

Composition title: _____

Things I did well in this composition:

_____

_____

_____

Things I need to work on in my next composition:

_____

_____

_____

Look at your *Progress Check* on page 128 of Chapter 6. How did you improve your writing in this composition?

_____

_____

_____

Responding to Nonfiction

Think about the last time you read a nonfiction article in a magazine. When you finished it, perhaps you decided to share your opinions about it with a friend. First, you probably summarized the article for your friend, and then you explained your opinions about it.

In this chapter, you will read a nonfiction selection and write a composition with a summary and response.

GETTING STARTED

A Read sample compositions

Each of the following sample compositions includes a summary and response to a nonfiction selection. As you read each composition, think about these questions.

1 Does the writer agree with the ideas in the selection?
2 What main points does the writer express and develop in the body?

Sample 1

Helpful Companions

"This Dog's Way with Words Turns Fetch into Child's Play" by Thomas Maugh is an article from the *Los Angeles Times* (June 11, 2004) about Rico, a dog that can fetch over 200 objects by name. When a person tells Rico to bring a certain object, he can do it with 93 percent accuracy. Rico can also use simple logic to identify objects. He demonstrates the same level of logic as a three-year-old human. These findings show that some animals may have more ability to understand language than we had previously thought.

I have often thought that dogs are more intelligent than most people think, so I'm glad to read about their ability to understand a large vocabulary. Because dogs are so smart, they're useful to humans in many ways. For example, police dogs help police officers do their jobs. They follow commands to find a person or even to attack when necessary. As another example, seeing-eye dogs provide a useful service to those who are sight-impaired. The dogs receive very specialized training to learn how to help sight-impaired people live independent lives. To give one more example, dogs provide help and companionship for elderly people who live alone. My eighty-year-old Aunt Edna lives by herself with her dog Deefer. Deefer has learned to bring items to her, such as her slippers, the TV remote control, and her purse. For my aunt, Deefer is a much-needed helper and companion. Because dogs are smart and able to learn verbal commands, they can serve humankind as useful workers and as helpful companions.

Sample 2

Tolerance and Table Manners

In "Be Appreciative, Act like a Pig" (*Los Angeles Times,* October 10, 1994), Norine Dresser shows how cultural differences in table manners can cause misunderstandings. Dresser gives an example of a man from the Philippines named Peter who is a guest in the home of his new American friends, the Gordons. The problem arises when Peter burps loudly at the end of his meal. The Americans think he is acting rudely, but Dresser explains that Peter is simply complimenting the good food. The fact is that table manners are different from culture to culture.

I believe that both sides, Peter and the Gordons, missed important points. On the one hand, the Gordons knew that their guest was from a different culture, so they should have expected some differences in table manners. On the other hand, Peter should have considered that he was in a new culture, and that he may have needed to change his behavior. In any case, in cross-cultural situations, people need to be more accepting and more sensitive to differences. In this way, they can avoid feeling uncomfortable because of cultural differences.

Adapted from a composition by Esteban Andiola

Sample 3

The True Victims of Smoking

"Smoking Parents Lost in Court" in *News for You* (December 1, 1993) tells about a court decision to protect a child against exposure to secondhand smoke. Elyse Tanner has asthma, and her parents'

continued

smoking has caused the girl many health problems. When the case went to court, the judge ruled against the parents, and Elyse went to live with her grandmother.

I agree with the court's decision because children should not be exposed to cigarettes in their homes. One reason is that secondhand smoke is harmful for everyone, especially children. In the article, a government expert states that secondhand smoke can cause ear problems, lung damage, and asthma in children. Most important, however, is that it seems obvious that the parents in this case are not interested in what is best for their child. How can they not know that their smoking is harmful to their asthmatic daughter? It seems obvious to me that the parents were not taking care of their child's health. Therefore, I believe the court made the right decision. It is not fair for children to suffer from health problems because of their parents' bad habits.

Adapted from a composition by Shahzedi Memon

Sample 4

In "Hyperhigh Tech" in *Bridges to Academic Writing* (1998) by Ann Strauch, the author describes her husband's enthusiasm for computerized devices and her own doubts about the value of high-tech electronics. She gives three examples. In the first example, she describes her husband's excitement over a computerized showerhead. The author argues that using your hands and the faucets will do the same job just as well or better. In the next example, the author argues that an old-fashioned coffee pot makes the same coffee that an automatic coffeemaker makes. In the last example, her husband wants to get a new DVD player, one with all the up-to-date technology, but the author argues that a fancy one has unnecessary features and makes day-to-day tasks too complicated.

Ms. Strauch and her husband are examples of how people love or hate technology. I am somewhere in between the two. I agree with the author that sometimes an electronic item becomes so complicated that it is annoying to use. For example, every time I need to program my video player to record a TV program at a certain time, I have to read the complicated directions. I believe that part of the problem is that modern electronics just have too many buttons and features. However, there are some computerized devices that do save time and make life more enjoyable. Ms. Strauch may not like complicated electronics, but in my opinion, there is nothing better than waking up to the smell of fresh coffee, prepared just minutes before my alarm goes off, thanks to my high-tech coffeemaker.

B Select a topic

Choose a short nonfiction selection to summarize from the list below. Choose a selection that you would like to express your opinion about. Be sure to write down reference information about your source.

1 An article from a newspaper or a magazine
2 An article from the Internet
3 The following selection

In Quest of True Equality

At a holiday party at work, Joe walks in with an average-looking brown-haired woman. Then a couple of minutes later, heads turn when Mickey walks in with a black-haired beauty. Why does everyone notice the beauty instead of the ordinary-looking woman? Could it be a case of appearance discrimination? Appearance discrimination is defined as "a failure to address or correct discrimination based on appearance, dress, or grooming."* (Pincus-Roth) Drawing on this definition, the situation at the holiday party seems to be such a case. This raises several questions. Are good-looking individuals always at an advantage over less attractive ones? If so, in what cases do these advantages (or disadvantages) occur? Most important, are we as a society the ultimate loser in the game of appearance discrimination?

In a recent article in the *Daily Princetonian,* Zach Pincus-Roth discusses appearance discrimination in some detail. He classifies it as an affirmative action* issue, an injustice that deserves protection by law. In his 1994 study, he found that "below-average looking people earned 5 to 10 percent less than average-looking people, who earned about 5 percent less than people with above-average looks." Furthermore, he refers to the "Equal Employment Opportunity Act of 1964, which banned* discrimination based on sex, race, ethnicity,* or national origin." Pincus-Roth suggests that appearance needs to be added to the previous list, because a person cannot control his or her appearance, and below-average looking people are at an economic disadvantage in the workplace.

I agree with Pincus-Roth. People's different levels of attractiveness do put them at an advantage or a disadvantage throughout their lives, and these different experiences influence who they are. Looking at my own life, I can see how I have enjoyed certain advantages among family and friends when compared to my older sister, who has a weight problem. I have grown up to be a much more social and likable person, while she has become shy, with occasional sad moods. However, I would not consider myself better than she is in any way. In fact, she has many fine qualities that I don't have.

On the other hand, my friend Kristin has experienced another type of appearance discrimination. Her attractiveness has actually put her at a disadvantage in her career. After graduation from a famous university a few years ago, she joined a major medical equipment firm and has been working hard to get a better position than her current position of administrative

continued

assistant. She is well qualified for a better position and has the education and experience to move up to a higher position. Unfortunately, because of her attractiveness, her bosses have thought of her as all beauty and no brains.

My sister and Kristin share the problem of appearance discrimination. The advantages and disadvantages of appearance discrimination may vary from situation to situation, but one thing is certain – society as a whole suffers due to appearance discrimination. Furthermore, the problem can only increase as the world becomes more crowded and competitive. In order for the world to become a better place for everyone, we need to work toward true equality. Only then can we truly become a planet of one people.

Work Cited

Pincus-Roth, Zach. "Look Again – Newest 'ism' Has Everyone Looking in the Mirror for Special Treatment." *Daily Princetonian,* September 20, 2000 <http://www.dailyprincetonian.com>.

by Aditi Srivastava

affirmative action: *an effort to improve employment and education opportunities for minority groups and women*
banned: *prohibited*
ethnicity: *cultural background*
grooming: *cleanliness and attention to physical appearance*

C Explore ideas

Do one of the following activities as a way to explore ideas and opinions about your selection.

1 Freewrite about your selection, writing down everything that comes to mind.
2 List ideas about your selection and group them into categories.

D Discuss your ideas with others

With a partner or in a small group, take turns telling about your selection.

1 Explain the most important ideas in the selection.
2 Express your opinion about the selection.
3 Ask others to give their opinions.

PREPARING THE FIRST DRAFT

A Make a rough outline

Using your notes from *Explore ideas* on the opposite page, make an outline similar to the one on the right. Write key words, phrases, and ideas.

I. MAIN IDEA Title Author or source General idea of selection
II. BODY Response Your opinions Details
III. CONCLUSION

B Compose the main idea

THE MAIN IDEA

In a composition about a nonfiction selection, a clear main idea sentence includes the title, the author or source, and the main idea of the selection. The title of the selection is in quotation marks. The name of a book, magazine, or newspaper is underlined. When a paper is typewritten, sometimes *italics* are used instead of underlining.

Title:	"Health Risks from Smoking More Widespread, Report Says"
Author:	James Gerstenzano
Source:	Los Angeles Times, May 28, 2004
General idea:	Smoking damages nearly every human organ and is increasingly a habit of the poorest Americans.
Main idea:	In the Los Angeles Times article "Health Risks from Smoking More Widespread, Report Says" (May 28, 2004), James Gerstenzano reports that smoking damages nearly every human organ and is increasingly a habit of the poorest Americans.

Practice 1

Select and read a newspaper article. Then write a main idea sentence for a composition.

Your turn ↜

Write the main idea for the selection you chose in *Explore ideas* on page 146.

C Write the body

ORGANIZING A RESPONSE TO NONFICTION

In a written response to nonfiction, you are free to use any logical method of organization that supports your opinion. For example, you might include examples, reasons, parallel points, a narration of a personal experience, or a combination of these.

Practice 2

Choose one of the sample compositions at the beginning of this chapter. Write your own opinion about the topic.

Your turn ↜

Write the body of your composition. Give a summary of your selection and then give your opinion in a response.

D Write a conclusion

THE CONCLUSION

The conclusion ties the entire composition together and gives closure. A good conclusion refers to the main idea of the selection and reminds the reader of the writer's strongest opinion.

Therefore, I believe the court made the right decision. It is not fair for children to suffer from health problems because of their parents' bad habits.

For my aunt, Deefer is a much-needed helper and companion. Because dogs are smart and able to learn verbal commands, they can serve humankind as useful workers and as helpful companions.

Read the composition below. Then choose the best conclusion. Discuss your choice with a partner.

"The Oval Bug Battles the New Beetle" by Kara Grace (*Our Voices*, 2003) describes the new version of the Volkswagen Beetle, informally known as the VW Bug. The original, oval-shaped Bug of the 1960s was popular because it offered economy in both purchase price and gas consumption. The VW Bug was the most popular economy car for many years, but it was last produced in Mexico in 2003. The updated Volkswagen Beetle has a new shape, a more powerful engine, and many modern luxuries.

It's good that Volkswagen has continued producing low-priced cars such as the Beetle, which costs under $18,000. Also, with an average of 26 miles per gallon of gas, the new Beetle offers reasonable gas economy. However, in the future, Volkswagen needs to follow Toyota's example and create a hybrid similar to the Toyota Prius, which runs on both gas and electricity. I have a Prius, and it gets an average of 45 miles per gallon in the city. It has reached as high as 52 miles per gallon on the highway. Superior gas economy is especially important, with gas prices rising and oil supplies that are sometimes undependable.

---

1 In my opinion, the Toyota Prius is the best car for gas economy.

2 Even though the new Beetle is a great car in many ways, Volkswagen needs to put gas economy first.

3 I don't understand why people continue to buy cars with poor gas economy.

Your turn

Write a conclusion for your composition.

E Put together the first draft

In this section you have written all the pieces that you need for a short composition: the main idea, the body, and the conclusion. Put these pieces together to create the first draft of your composition. You will add a title in the next section.

III REVISING YOUR WRITING

A Write a suitable title

> **TITLES**
>
> The title for a summary and response composition should represent the most important idea in the entire composition. Often, the most important idea focuses on your response to the selection.
>
> Sample composition 1, written in response to "This Dog's Way with Words Turns Fetch into Child's Play," was titled "Helpful Companions."

Practice 4

Reread the composition about the new Volkswagen Beetle in *Practice 3* on page 149. Then choose the best title from the list below.

1 Volkswagens
2 Low-Priced Cars
3 Superior Gas Economy
4 Volkswagen's New Beetle
5 The Toyota Prius

Your turn

Write a title for your composition.

B Benefit from peer feedback

Exchange drafts with a partner. Read your partner's draft and check it using the *Revision Checklist* below. At this point, do not check grammar. Then give your partner feedback.

> **REVISION CHECKLIST** ☑
>
> ☐ 1 Does the draft have any places that are unclear?
>
> ☐ 2 Is the draft organized clearly, according to the outline form on page 147?
>
> ☐ 3 Is the response well developed with plenty of specific, supporting details?
>
> ☐ 4 Does the draft have a suitable title?

C Make revision decisions

Using the *Revision Checklist,* decide on changes you want to make. Mark the changes in your first draft.

D Write the second draft

Write the second draft of your composition.

IV EDITING YOUR WRITING

A Edit for sentence fragments

SENTENCE FRAGMENTS

A sentence fragment is an incomplete sentence.

- Sometimes a sentence fragment is missing a subject or verb.

  One more point.

To correct this type of fragment, add a subject and/or verb.

  S   V
  He mentioned one more point.

- A dependent clause that stands alone is a sentence fragment because it is an incomplete thought.

  Because violence on TV can cause children to behave violently.

To correct this type of fragment, a dependent clause needs to be joined to an independent clause to become a complete thought. If the dependent clause is at the end of the sentence, it does not take a comma. If it comes first, use a comma before the independent clause.

  Parents need to select what their children watch on TV because violence on TV can cause children to behave violently.

  Because violence on TV can cause children to behave violently, parents need to select what their children watch on TV.

Practice 5

Edit the following composition for sentence fragments. First, put a check (✓) at the beginning of each independent clause. Next, join each dependent clause fragment to the appropriate independent clause. The beginning of the exercise has been done for you.

¹✓"Take the Shock Out of Culture Shock" by Charlotte Thomas explains the discomfort that study-abroad students experience in their new cultural environments. ²✓Culture shock affects most study-abroad students in one way or another. ³Because the students' basic assumptions about day-to-day living are no longer reliable. ⁴They can't predict what's going to happen in social situations. ⁵This discomfort will pass, however. ⁶After the student adjusts to a new way of life. ⁷Also, reverse culture shock can be a problem. ⁸When the student returns home. ⁹Ms. Thomas offers solutions to reduce culture shock. ¹⁰Such as learning about the new culture, keeping in touch with family and friends, and making new friends in the new culture.

¹¹I know that both culture shock and reverse culture shock can be a problem. ¹²Because I have experienced both. ¹³I lived in Colombia. ¹⁴For almost two years. ¹⁵When I was in my twenties. ¹⁶Luckily for me, I adjusted fairly easily to living in Colombia. ¹⁷Because I had studied the language and culture. ¹⁸Also, I made friends in Colombia, and my family and friends from home visited me. ¹⁹On the other hand, I wasn't prepared for reverse culture shock. ²⁰Because nobody had told me about it. ²¹I noticed it while I was still in Colombia. ²²I became so worried when I read the newspapers about horrible things happening at home. ²³Such as murders, terrible accidents, and political problems. ²⁴After I arrived home, I wanted to talk about my life in Colombia, but people were more interested in other things. ²⁵I felt like I was not part of my friends' lives anymore. ²⁶It took a while to adjust and fit in again. ²⁷It's good that Ms. Thomas is emphasizing both culture shock and reverse culture shock in her advice to study-abroad students.

Work Cited

Thomas, Charlotte. "Take the Shock Out of Culture Shock." *Peterson's*, March 21, 2004 <http://www.petersons.com/stdyabrd/abroad4.html>.

B Benefit from peer feedback

Meet with a partner and exchange drafts. Read your partner's draft, and check for sentence fragments.

C Write the final draft

As you write your final draft, make the revisions and edits you have noted on your second draft.

V FOLLOWING UP

A Share your writing

Before you turn in your final draft, do one of these activities to share your writing.

1 Small Group Read-Around (page 35)
2 Traveling Compositions (page 55)
3 Writing to a Classmate (page 73)

B Check your progress

After you get your composition back from your instructor, complete the *Progress Check*.

PROGRESS CHECK

Date: _____

Composition title: _____

Things I did well in this composition:

_____

_____

_____

Things I need to work on in my next composition:

_____

_____

_____

Look at your *Progress Checks* in the previous chapters. Compare those charts with the chart on this page. How did you improve your writing in this composition?

_____

_____

_____

Critiquing
Fiction

Have you recently finished reading a short story or other selection in fiction, and then wanted to tell a friend about it? First, you probably summarized the story for your friend and then you shared your opinions about it.

In this chapter, you will read a selection of fiction and write a summary and response based on it.

A Read sample compositions

Read the two fiction selections, which are each followed by a sample critique. In a critique, the writer summarizes a selection and then gives his or her opinion about it. After you read the critiques, answer these questions.

1 What are the writer's opinions about the selection?
2 How does the writer support and develop his or her ideas?

Selection 1

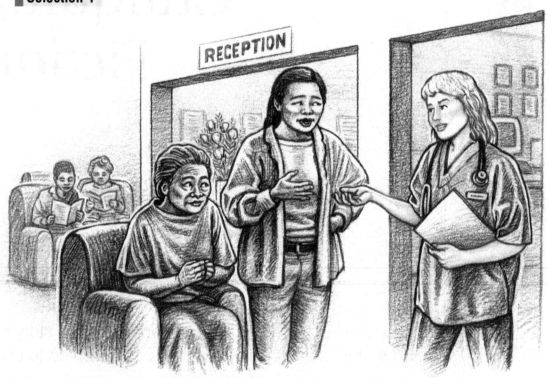

The following selection is an excerpt from April and the Dragon Lady *by Lensey Namioka. The novel is set in the United States and focuses on the relationship between April and her Chinese grandmother. In this scene April is taking her grandmother to see the doctor. This is her grandmother's first visit to a doctor in the United States.*

I gave Grandma's name to the receptionist, and we were told to take a seat in the waiting room. The magazines were all old, and in any case, Grandma wouldn't read magazines in English.

A young nurse came out into the waiting room. "May? Is May here?" she asked, looking around the room.

When nobody answered, she looked at the card in her hand. "My?" she tried.

Still no one responded. The nurse's glance came to Grandma. "Are you May? Or My? Er . . . maybe I'm not pronouncing your name right."

"My grandmother's name is Mei-yun Chen. Is she the one you're looking for?"

The nurse smiled with relief. "She sure is. So I got it right the first time." She looked down at Grandma. "Come in with me, May."

I remembered the respectful way everybody addressed Grandma at her birthday party: Grandma Chen or Auntie Chen by the younger generations, and Mrs. Chen by those of her own generation. Only very close friends, like Mrs. Liang, were allowed to call her Mei-yun. Even though Grandma was acting funny lately, she was still entitled* to her dignity. It seemed disrespectful for this young nurse to address Grandma by her first name and to get it wrong, too.

"My grandmother's given name is not May," I said firmly to the nurse. It's Mei-yun. But please call her Mrs. Chen."

The nurse continued to smile brightly. "I know you people have your own customs, but it's our policy here to use first names. We feel more comfortable with that."

The condescending* way she talked really grated on me*. "*You* may feel more comfortable with first names, but how do your patients feel?"

I was talking to air. The nurse was already leading Grandma down the corridor. Fuming,* I got up and followed. At the door to the doctor's office, the nurse asked me to wait outside. "While your grandmother is seeing Dr. Wilton, can you fill out these forms for us? We need some information since this is her first visit."

I looked at Grandma's face, which seemed to be showing signs of panic. "I think I should go inside with her," I said. "My grandmother doesn't speak much English."

"That's all right," the nurse assured me. "She doesn't need to."

Before I could say another word, the door to the doctor's office shut in my face. I took the forms the nurse gave me and sat down on a chair in the waiting room. I knew immediately that I couldn't answer half the questions on the sheet. For a start, I didn't know her maiden name* or how many siblings* she had. Nor did I have a clue* about her medical history.

I finally decided to fill in the answers that I knew and then ask Grandma about the rest. Just as I was putting away my ballpoint pen, the nurse came out and rushed up to me. "Can you come with me? We're having a little trouble with your grandmother."

"What's the matter?" I asked, as we hurried to the examination room.

"The only thing she'll let us do is take her blood pressure," said the nurse. "But she won't get undressed! Dr. Wilton can't examine her unless she gets undressed."

entitled: *had the right to*
condescending: *treating someone with an air of superiority*
grated on me: *bothered me*
fuming: *angrily*
maiden name: *original unmarried name of a woman*
siblings: *brothers and/or sisters*
clue: *idea*

Critique of Selection 1

Intercultural Awareness and Respect

The excerpt from the novel *April and the Dragon Lady* by Lensey Namioka is about April and her Chinese grandmother's first visit to a doctor in the United States. In the waiting room, the nurse insists on calling Grandma by her first name. April wants her grandmother to be treated more respectfully, as older people are treated in China. When it's time for Grandma to see the doctor, the nurse won't allow April to go with Grandma. In the middle of Grandma's examination by the doctor, the nurse has to ask for April's help because Grandma doesn't speak English.

The nurse in this excerpt is unkind, and that may be because she doesn't understand cultural differences. Fortunately, I believe that most nurses are more sensitive than the nurse in this story. The real point of this excerpt, however, is that in the United States, senior citizens are not treated with the same kind of respect as they are in Asia.

Based on my own experience, I believe this is true. My grandmother was Filipino, and when she came to the United States, she was not treated with the same respect as in her native Manila. People often ignored her when she spoke to them. When she went shopping, clerks did not serve her right away, and sometimes they spoke to her casually. Not only that, but her American-born grandchildren did not treat her as respectfully as her grandchildren did in Manila. When she took care of them, they did not speak to her politely or obey her. She must not have felt very respected. I hope that people become more aware of cultural differences so that older people from other cultures will feel more welcomed and respected.

Selection 2

The City Man and the Fisherman

A successful businessman from the city visited a small village next to the sea. One morning he decided take a walk along the beach. His time was very limited, though, because he had to make several important business calls. He stepped quickly and nervously as he thought about the all the business obligations he had to take care of.

After a short time, the city man came across a fisherman sitting on the sand. The fisherman was watching his small boat bobbing up and down in the water and the birds circling lazily in the sky above. The city man stopped and began a conversation with the fisherman.

"Good morning," he said as he approached the fisherman who was still sitting on the sand and enjoying the beautiful scenery. The fisherman nodded a return greeting.

"Excuse me," continued the city man. "Why are you sitting on the sand? Why aren't you out fishing?"

"I caught all the fish I need for today," replied the fisherman.

"Oh, but let me give you some good advice," the city man told him. "If you fish for more than your normal amount, you will make more money."

"Why should I make more money?" yawned the fisherman.

"Well, you would be able to buy more things, such as a bigger boat," smiled the city man. He patted his expensive clothing as he spoke and nodded toward the fisherman's small boat.

"Why do I need a bigger boat?" questioned the puzzled fisherman.

"Obviously," said the city man, "if you have a bigger boat, then you can catch even more fish, and you can even hire a crew to work for you. You can be the boss and wear expensive clothing."

"Why should I do that?" frowned the fisherman. "Then I'd have to work twice as hard as I work now. Maybe three times as hard. And expensive clothing is certainly no more comfortable than what I wear now." He looked down at his simple, but comfortable clothing.

"Oh, you foolish man!" laughed the city man. "If you followed my advice, then you would earn so much money that when you were ready to retire, you could do anything with your time you wanted to do!"

The fisherman looked back up at the birds contentedly flying around in wide circles and diving into the water for an occasional fish.

"But that's what I'm already doing," he smiled without looking back at the city man.

Critique of Selection 2

A Modern Folktale About Work

The modern folktale "The City Man and the Fisherman" is about opposite viewpoints on work and life satisfaction. The successful businessman from the city tells the simple fisherman that he should work harder to prepare for retiring to a life of leisure. The life the city man describes, however, is one of more and more work. The fisherman answers that he doesn't need to work hard for a happy future because he is already happy with his life. He is satisfied with his job, and he has enough leisure time to enjoy a comfortable life. The lesson of this folktale is that people who are only concerned with work and earning money can lose sight of real life satisfaction.

It's true that people who build their whole lives around work may lose the chance to enjoy some of its pleasures. But it's also true that happiness means different things to different people. Some people get great pleasure from work. For others, their lives outside of work give them the most pleasure. Perhaps the real message is that each person must find his or her own balance of work and leisure.

Another point is important as well. The city man believes that the fisherman needs his advice. But the fisherman is perfectly happy with his life as it is. He doesn't need the city man's advice about happiness. All in all, however, this modern folktale makes its central point fairly clear: job success and hard work don't always lead to happiness.

B Select a topic

Read the following selections and discuss with a partner the questions that follow each selection. Then choose which selection you will critique.

Selection 1

The following is an excerpt from the novel Hatchet *by Gary Paulsen.*

Brian Robeson stared out the window of the small plane at the endless green northern wilderness below. It was a small plane, a Cessna 406 – a bush plane – and the engine was so loud, so roaring and consuming and loud, that it ruined any chance for conversation.

Not that he had much to say. He was . . . the only passenger on the plane with a pilot named – what was it? Jim or Jake or something – who was in his mid-forties, and he had been silent as he worked to prepare for takeoff. In fact, since Brian had come – driven by his mother – to the small airport in Hampton, New York to meet the plane, the pilot had spoken only five words to him.

"Get in the copilot's seat."

Which Brian had done. They had taken off and that was the last of the conversation. There had been the initial excitement, of course. He had never flown in a single-engine plane before, and to be sitting in the copilot's seat with all the controls right there in front of him, all the instruments in his face as the plane clawed* for altitude, jerking* and sliding on the wind currents as the pilot took off, had been interesting and exciting. But in five minutes they had leveled off at six thousand feet and headed northwest, and from then on the pilot had been silent, staring out the front, and the drone* of the engine had been all that was left. The drone and the sea of green trees that lay before the plane's nose and flowed to the horizon, spread with lakes, swamps,* and wandering streams and rivers. . . .

The pilot sat large, his hands lightly on the wheel, feet on the rudder pedals.* He seemed more a machine than a man, an extension of the plane. On the dashboard* in front of him, Brian saw sundials, switches, meters, knobs, levers, cranks, lights, handles that were wiggling* and flickering,* all indicating nothing that he understood, and the pilot seemed the same way. Part of the plane, not human.

When he saw Brian look at him, the pilot seemed to open up a bit and he smiled. "Ever fly in the copilot's seat before?" He leaned over and lifted the headset off his right ear and put it on his temple,* yelling to overcome the sound of the engine.

Brian shook his head. He had never been in any kind of plane, never seen the cockpit* of a plane except in films or on television. It was loud and confusing. "First time."

"It's not as complicated as it looks. Good plane like this almost flies itself." The pilot shrugged.* "Makes my job easy." He took Brian's left arm. "Here, put your hands on the controls, your feet on the rudder pedals, and I'll show you what I mean."

Brian shook his head. "I'd better not."

"Sure. Try it . . ."

Brian reached out and took the wheel in a grip so tight his knuckles* were white. He pushed his feet down on the pedals. The plane slewed* suddenly to the right.

"Not so hard. Take her light, take her light."

Brian eased off, relaxing his grip. . . . The vibration of the plane came through the wheel and the pedals. It seemed almost alive.

"See?" The pilot let go of his wheel, raised his hands in the air and took his feet off the pedals to show Brian he was actually flying the plane alone.

clawed: *struggled to go up*
cockpit: *area in the front of an airplane where the pilot sits*
dashboard: *front panel with control instruments*
drone: *low, humming sound*
flickering: *shining on and off*
jerking: *moving suddenly*
knuckles: *joints of the fingers*
rudder pedals: *foot levers for steering*
shrugged: *lifted and lowered his shoulders*
slewed: *curved*
swamps: *wetlands*
temple: *side of the face above the cheekbone*
wiggling: *moving quickly from side to side*

1 How do you think Brian felt when he was actually flying the plane?
2 How would you feel in his situation?
3 Think of a situation in which you did something new and exciting. Describe this situation to your partner, using as many details as possible.

The following selection is from Shizuko's Daughter *by Kyoko Mori. The scene takes place in Masa's garden. Yuki, her granddaughter, is visiting during a summer vacation from college. Masa wants to discuss Yuki's future with her.*

Masa walked slowly toward the house, stopping now and then to snip off dead leaves or fading flowers, pull out the weeds growing between the plants. There were few weeds. The drought* had killed those that had sprung up* after Yuki's visit. Yuki had spent hours of her two-week visit weeding the flowerbeds and vegetable plots. Masa wondered if Yuki had spent so much of her time outside because she wanted to avoid talking to her.

But Yuki must have been anxious to see us, Masa told herself. She had visited in the last weeks of June, as soon as her college was out for the summer. She said she wanted to stay longer but couldn't because she had to work. Besides, she needed to use the studio at her college for photography and she had to go to the library to read.

"Why do you have to read books or even go to college to study art?" Masa had asked her. "I thought you would be able to learn just from doing it on your own. Isn't that how all the great artists learned? They didn't go to college."

Yuki shook her head. "That was a different time, and a lot of them were apprenticed* to other artists even then. They didn't just teach themselves everything. It's hard to explain."

"I was thinking you could live with us all year round and still be an artist. This is a nice quiet place to live. Why not?"

"I don't know. How would I support myself here?"

"You wouldn't have to worry about that. Grandpa's pension* is enough for all three of us if we live modestly.* If you want to work, you can always give lessons."

"But I don't want to spend a long time looking at kids' drawings."

"You can coach the track* team at the village school. Even people around here read about you in the papers last year when you won those competitions."

"I don't want to coach track teams."

"What will you do after you graduate, anyway? Will you become a teacher somewhere else then?"

"Grandma, I don't know." Yuki sighed. "I just started college. I don't know what I'll do afterward."

"What is the use of going to college if you don't know what you're going there for?"

"Maybe I'm going *because* I don't know. I just want to study art now. I have no idea about four years from now or even next year. I don't want to think that far ahead."

Masa was going to point out that this was too haphazard* a way to live when Yuki abruptly stood up and put on her straw hat.

"I'm going to the garden. I didn't weed your petunia patch yet," she said. "Let me know if there's something else I can do."

Yuki was never rude or irritable on this visit. Even when they disagreed, her face was always full of patience. But something was wrong. Masa felt a strain* when they talked, and she was sure that Yuki felt it also.

apprenticed: *working for an expert to learn a particular skill*
drought: *a long period of time with little rain*
haphazard: *without a plan, not organized*
modestly: *not expensively*
pension: *salary for a retired person*
sprung up: *grown quickly*
strain: *feeling of discomfort between people*
track: *field sports, such as running and jumping*

1 What is Masa worried about? What does she want Yuki to do? Why?
2 What are Yuki's concerns? Why?
3 In the last paragraph, what does "strain" refer to?
4 Masa and Yuki have very different views about college. Which point of view do you agree with more? Why?
5 Are your reasons for being in school similar to or different from Yuki's? Explain.

The following selection is titled The Wooden Chest. *It is an old folktale that contains wisdom for all ages.*

There was once an old woman who had lost her husband and lived all alone. She had worked hard all her life, raising a family and taking in extra work as a seamstress. Now, in her old age, bad luck left her penniless. Old and bent, she was unable to take care of herself any longer. Her hands trembled too much to thread a needle, and her vision blurred too much for her to make a straight stitch.

The old woman had two sons and two daughters, but they were all grown and married now, and they were busy with their own lives. They only had time to stop by to see their mother once a week.

Gradually, the old woman grew more and more feeble,* and her children came by to see her less and less. "They don't want to be around me at all any more," she told herself, "because they're so busy with their own lives and afraid I'll become a burden."* She stayed up all night worrying about what would become of her, until at last she thought of a plan.

The next morning the old woman went to see her neighbor, a carpenter, and asked him to give her a large, old chest that he didn't need any longer. Then she went to see another neighbor, a locksmith, and asked him to give her an old lock. Finally, she went to see still another neighbor, a glass blower, and asked him for all the unusable old broken pieces of glass that he had.

The old woman took the chest home, filled it to the top with the broken glass, locked it up tight, and put it under her kitchen table. The next time her children came to visit, they sat at the table and bumped their feet against it.

"What's in this chest?" they asked, looking under the table.

"Oh, nothing," the old woman replied, "just some things I've been saving."

The four children pushed at it with their feet and noticed how heavy it was. They kicked it and heard a rattling noise inside. "It must be full of all the gold she's inherited and saved over the years," they whispered to one another.

So they talked it over and decided they needed to guard the treasure. They made a plan to take turns living with the old woman, and they could look after her, too. In this way, the old woman always had one of her children living with her and helping her. This went on for some time.

At last the old woman grew sick and died. Her children gave her a very nice funeral, for they knew that a great fortune sat under the kitchen table, and they could afford to spend some money on the old woman now.

When the service was over, the four children hunted through the house until they found the key. Eagerly, they unlocked the chest. And, of course, they found it full of broken glass.

"What a rotten trick!" yelled the oldest child. "What a cruel thing to do to your own children!"

"But what else could she have done, really?" asked the next child. "We must be honest with ourselves. If it wasn't for this chest, we would have neglected our dear mother until the end of her days."

"I'm so ashamed of myself," sobbed the next child.

"And so am I," moaned the last child. "We forced our own mother to use a trick to get our help."

The oldest child pushed the chest over to make sure there was nothing valuable hidden among the glass after all. He poured the broken pieces out until it was entirely empty.

Then the four children stared silently at the floor for a long time.

burden: *a difficult duty or responsibility*
feeble: *weak*

1 What are the old woman's concerns? What does she want from her children? Explain.
2 What are the concerns of the children? What do they want? Explain.
3 What's your opinion about the method the mother used to get her children's help?
4 How is the woman taken care of in this story? How does this compare with how senior citizens are treated in your culture?

C Explore ideas

Do one of these activities as a way to explore ideas about your selection.

1 Freewrite about your selection, writing down everything that comes to mind.

2 List ideas about your selection and group them into categories.

D Discuss your ideas with others

With a partner or in a small group, follow these steps to tell about your selection.

1 Briefly summarize what the selection is about and what happened.

2 Express your opinion about the selection. What did you like or not like about it? Have you been in a similar situation?

3 Answer any questions your classmates have.

II PREPARING THE FIRST DRAFT

A Make a rough outline

Using ideas from your freewriting or list in *Explore ideas*, make an outline similar to the one on the right. Then complete it writing key words, phrases, and ideas.

I. MAIN IDEA
Title
Author or source
General idea of selection

II. SUMMARY
Who the selection is about
What happened

III. CRITIQUE
Your opinions and response

IV. CONCLUSION

B Compose the main idea

THE MAIN IDEA SENTENCE OF A CRITIQUE

The first sentence of a critique of a work of fiction includes the title of the selection, the author or source, and the main or general idea of the selection. In a handwritten piece of writing, the name of a book should be underlined. However, when it is written on a computer, the name of a book should be written in *italics*. The title of a short story, movie, or show is written in quotation marks.

> The novel *Caramelo* by Sandra Cisneros is about the colorful life of the Reyes family as they move from Mexico City to make a new life in Chicago.
>
> The movie "The Terminal" with Tom Hanks tells the story of a man who has to live in an airport terminal because he does not have proper identification to enter the country.
>
> In one episode of the classic TV comedy "I Love Lucy," Lucy gets into trouble when she works in a candy factory.

Practice 1

Think of a movie or TV drama you have seen recently. Write the main idea for the story. Then in a small group, read your main idea.

Your turn ↜

Write the main idea of the fiction piece you have selected for your composition.

C Summarize and critique the selection

SUMMARY AND CRITIQUE

For the summary, give the essential ideas from the selection using your own words, and leaving out nonessential details. The summary should be brief compared to the critique. As a reminder, in most cases, the literary present tense is used in a summary.

For the critique, use any logical method of organization that fits your ideas.
- Discuss the characters in the selection, organizing with parallel points.
- Narrate your own personal experience in one part of the critique.
- Give examples.
- Express your personal opinions, giving reasons for your opinions.

Practice 2

Form a small group. Briefly summarize and give your critique of the movie or drama you chose in *Practice 1*.

Your turn 🔗

Write the body of your composition. Start with a summary of your selection and then give your critique.

D Write a conclusion

> ### THE CONCLUSION
>
> The conclusion ties the entire composition – both summary and critique – together and gives closure. This can be done in one or more ways.
> - Restate your most important opinion.
> - Make a suggestion that grows out of the summary and critique.
> - Summarize your reactions to the selection.

Practice 3

Continuing with the same movie or TV drama you talked about in the previous practices, write a conclusion for your summary and critique. Share your conclusion with a partner or in a small group.

Your turn 🔗

Write a clear conclusion to provide closure for your composition.

E Put together the first draft

In this section you have written all the pieces that you need for a short composition: the main idea, the body, and the conclusion. Put these pieces together to create the first draft of your composition. Then add a title.

A Develop your critique with details

USING DETAILS

Be sure to develop your ideas in the critique with plenty of specific, supporting details. Here are a few ways to do that.

- Use details from the selection to explain and support your points.
- Use supporting details from your own experience.
- Include brief quotations that strengthen your viewpoints. If you use a direct quotation, make sure you punctuate it correctly, with quotation marks before and after the quotation.

Practice 4

Read the following two student compositions. Then answer the questions on page 170.

Composition A

Death and God

"The Appointment in Samarra" by W. Somerset Maugham tells about a servant in Baghdad who tries to run away from Death. In this story, Death appears as a person who bumps into the servant in the marketplace. The terrified servant escapes to Samarra. Later, the master sees Death in the marketplace, and Death tells the master that he was surprised to see the servant in Baghdad because he had an appointment with him that night in Samarra. The story shows Maugham's belief in fate. The servant couldn't escape from Death, even though he tried his best to. I agree with the author's idea that our lives are in the hands of forces beyond our control because I believe that my life is controlled by God.

To give an example of how my life is not under my control, when I drive on the freeway, I don't know if I will have an accident because I can't control the other drivers. Also, if I fly to Mexico next month, something could happen that would affect my trip. I could get sick, or the flight could be delayed. Last, I have no idea how many years I will live. I take care of my health, but that's no guarantee of a long life. In reality, so many things are completely out of our control.

Also, I enjoyed the humor in the story because of the surprise ending and because of the imaginary figure of Death. Even though Death is just a creative touch to the story, the idea of fate, or God, as the controller of our lives is absolutely real.

Adapted from a composition by Rosa Maria Aguilar

1 In the second paragraph, how many examples does the author give to support her opinion that her life is not under her control?

2 Which transition signals does the author use to introduce her examples?

3 What specific details does the author include to support each of her examples?

Composition B

Fate or Free Will?

W. Somerset Maugham's "The Appointment in Samarra" is a story about one man's fate. A servant tries to avoid his time of death, but he unknowingly sends himself to his own death. Obviously, the author believes in fate – that everyone has his or her own predetermined destiny. I do not agree with this because I believe in free will, as my life experiences demonstrate.

In 1954 my family moved from North to South Vietnam because we disagreed with the Communist government. We did not accept a fate controlled by Communism. Unfortunately, in 1975 South Vietnam fell to the Communists. I was forced into a reeducation camp, where my family was poorly treated. Even this sad time of our lives did not convince us to accept a fate we didn't believe in, so in 1979, my family escaped to the United States. I followed them later, and we were reunited in 1991. Living here, we have more opportunities in business and education. We successfully changed our fate.

Another reason I believe that we can control our fate is that scientific research has helped humankind to prevent or cure several dangerous illnesses such as cancer, heart disease, polio, the plague, and cholera. In the past people with these diseases had to accept their fate and await death. Now, they have a choice about their health and their future.

Maugham's story is entertaining because of the ironic ending, but I don't believe in fate at all. I decide my own future.

Adapted from a composition by Thuong Phung

1 What two reasons does the author give to support his opinion?

2 What transition signal does the author use to introduce his second reason?

3 What specific details does the author include to explain what he means by "dangerous illnesses"?

Your turn ↶

Look at your draft. Do you include examples from your own experience and supporting details? Add to your draft as needed.

B Benefit from peer feedback

Exchange drafts with a partner. Read your partner's draft and check it using the *Revision Checklist* below. At this point, do not check grammar. Then give your partner feedback.

REVISION CHECKLIST ☑

- ☐ 1 Is the draft organized clearly, according to the outline form on page 166?
- ☐ 2 Is the summary short and written in the writer's own words?
- ☐ 3 Does the critique contain clear, well-developed opinions, with plenty of specific, supporting details?
- ☐ 4 If the critique contains direct quotes from the selection, are the quotes brief, and do they clearly support the writer's opinions?

C Make revision decisions

Using the *Revision Checklist,* decide on changes you want to make and mark them in your draft in your draft.

D Write the second draft

Write the second draft of your composition.

A Edit for correct modals

MODALS

Modals are commonly used in critiques, especially when the writer is making logical guesses about the characters in the selection, the author's intentions, or what might happen in the future. After a modal, use the simple form of the main verb.

Here are the most common uses of modals.

- Possibility: *may, might, could*

  It's true that people who build their whole lives around work <u>may</u> miss out on life's pleasures.

  Some <u>might</u> say that the city man is unable to see that the fisherman is happy with his life.

  If I fly to Mexico next month, something <u>could</u> happen that would affect my trip.

- Ability: *can*

  If the fisherman wants advice, he <u>can</u> ask for it.

- Necessity: *must*

  Perhaps the real message is that each person <u>must</u> find his or her own balance of work and leisure.

- Future: *will*

  I hope that people <u>will</u> become more aware of cultural differences.

- Advice or duty: *should*

  I believe that we <u>should</u> treat older people with more respect.

- Logical conclusion: *must*

  My grandmother <u>must</u> not have felt very respected.

Practice 5

Fill in the missing modals in the following composition. There may be more than one correct answer.

The Sadness of Good-bye

The excerpt from the novel *Paradise of the Blind* by Duong Thu Hyuong is about saying good-bye to loved ones. In the first scene, two lovers are parting in a train station in Russia. In the second scene, a young woman is leaving her family immediately after the fall of South Vietnam to start a new life as a refugee in the United States.

Even though both scenes are about parting, the circumstances are very different. I _____ see the first scene clearly in my
                                    (1)
mind. The lovers _____ see each other again. They
                        (2)
_____ miss each other very much, but it's almost certain that
        (3)
they _____ see each other again.
            (4)
I _____ only imagine the second scene. The young
        (5)
woman and her family _____ have very mixed feelings. They
                                (6)
_____ be happy for the chance for a new life. On the other
        (7)
hand, they _____ be sad because they _____
                (8)   (9)
not see each other for a long time.

Ms. Duong's good-bye scenes are very touching, especially the second one. I believe that the young woman _____ write to her family often
                                                    (10)
and plan for their reunion, and her family in Vietnam _____
                                                                (11)
never lose hope.

Practice 6

Read the following composition, based on a short story by Isaac Asimov. Find and correct the errors. There are 9 errors with the modal + simple form of the main verb. There are 3 errors related to literary present tense.

The Future: A Computer with Emotions?

¹The story "Key Item" by Isaac Asimov is about a team of scientists trying to find out why a computer is not working. ²Because this was an important computer, it musts be fixed soon, but nobody can comes up with the solution. ³After the scientists argue about it for a while, one of them figures out the problem. ⁴The computer wanted the scientists to include "please" in their commands to it. ⁵Once they say "please," the computer started working perfectly.

⁶I think Asimov wants to say that computers may becoming so advanced that one day in the future humans will to lose the ability to control them. ⁷Of course, no one can knows the future, but I think it's a fascinating idea to imagine that computers might eventually becomes so smart. ⁸Perhaps this will happen because computers can storing a lot of information, and they must to perform many functions that are amazingly human-like. ⁹Who knows? ¹⁰Maybe one day they will to think and feel like humans. ¹¹In any case, the story has given me something to think about.

Adapted from a composition by Virginia Macias

B Benefit from peer feedback

Meet with a partner and exchange drafts. As you read your partner's draft, check for the correct use of modals. Discuss any possible errors.

C Write the final draft

As you write your final draft, make the revisions and edits you have noted. Check for the correct use of modals.

V FOLLOWING UP

A Share your writing

Before you turn in your final draft, do one of these activities to share your writing.

1 Small Group Read-Around (page 35)
2 Traveling Compositions (page 55)
3 Responding to Your Classmates' Writing (page 73)

B Check your progress

After you get your composition back from your instructor, complete the *Progress Check* below.

PROGRESS CHECK

Date: _____

Composition title: _____

Things I did well in this composition:

_____

_____

_____

Things I need to work on in my next composition:

_____

_____

_____

Look at your *Progress Checks* in the previous chapters. How has your writing improved in this composition?

_____

_____

_____

Credits

TEXT CREDITS

Page 130: "One at a Time," from *Chicken Soup for the Soul* by Jack Canfield and Mark V. Hansen, 1993. Reprinted with the permission of Health Communications, Inc., Deerfield Beach, Florida.

Page 131: Adapted from "Why Mona Lisa Smiles" by Dianne Partie Lange, Los Angeles Times, April 14, 2003. Courtesy of the author.

Page 156: Excerpted from *April and the Dragon Lady* by Lensey Namioka, 1994. Reprinted with the permission of Harcourt, Inc., Orlando, Florida.

Page 160: Excerpted from *Hatchet* by Gary Paulsen, published by Aladdin Paperbacks, 1987. Reprinted with the permission of Atheneum Books for Young Readers, an imprint of Simon & Schuster Children's Publishing Division.

Page 162: Excerpted from *Shizuko's Daughter* by Kyoko Mori, published by Ballantine Books, 1993. Reprinted with the permission of Henry Holt & Company.